three birds

RENOVATIONS

Dream Home How-To

BONNIE  **ERIN** **LANA**
HINDMARSH   CAYLESS   TAYLOR

murdoch books

Sydney | London

three birds
RENOVATIONS
Dream Home How-To

Introduction 6

CHAPTER ONE

Colour me HAMPTONS 10

CHAPTER TWO

Mediterranean FARMHOUSE 40

CHAPTER THREE

The bold EXTENSION 80

CHAPTER FOUR

Contemporary COTTAGE 102

CHAPTER FIVE

Australian STAYCATION **136**

CHAPTER SIX

Three Birds HQ **182**

CHAPTER SEVEN

Christmas with THE BIRDS **194**

BONUS CHAPTER

Reno School ROCK STARS **212**

Index **250**
Thank you **254**

WE'RE BACK, BABY!

If you're thinking, *There's no way these three have come up with enough new tips to fill another book*, spoiler alert: we totally have! This book is packed to the faux rafters with hundreds of shiny new tips, DIY hacks galore and more design inspo than you can poke a palm frond at.

In fact, we've learned SO much more since completing Bon's home (which is where our last book left off). We've reworked more floor plans, knocked down more walls, prettied up more pergolas – basically, we've been doing all of the reno-y things the three of us love doing, and getting them done on schedule *and* within budget (shout-out to Ez for that). Each new project presents unique challenges, but that's exactly why we keep renovating: if the learnings keep coming, we keep sharing them.

We love mixing up our projects to keep things fresh, so alongside our whole home transformations we've also got an office revamp and two big, new builds for you. But as much as we love the thrill of building a new house from the ground up, the heart and soul of Three Birds Renovations remains renovating the much-loved suburban family home. We share some amazing transformations in this book, and it's hard to pick a favourite as we love them all.

To keep the reno magic rolling, we've needed lots of support, so we've welcomed many new birdies into our growing Three Birds nest, including a CEO, Candice (#bigbird). We are blown away that this business of

ours – this idea shared between three best friends in a café years ago – has grown into the company it has. Defying the odds, our business and our friendship continue to thrive, and both are doing better than ever. #bffs #workwives

Chapter 6 is dedicated to our nest – Three Birds HQ. It's where all of our birdies flock together, so it was a very special project. More than anything, we wanted our office to feel like a home away from home. And then, in a case of life imitating art, COVID hit, and the world found itself working from home anyway. Nowadays, you need only style the snippet you can see in the background of your Zoom screen! #ministylingmoment

For years, we've been preaching that how you FEEL in your home is the single most important thing, and now that we're all spending so much time at home, this message is more relevant than ever. This is why every project we do – from a bedroom makeover to a whole home reno – starts with the same question: how do we want to *feel* in this space? Once we know the answer, we find inspo pics and images of homes, spaces and places that match the feeling we're going for, and we use them to build a vision board. A vision board becomes your guiding light, your true north, and you will be able to refer back to it for EVERY design decision you make.

Every single project in this book had a rock-solid vision board. There's a whole chapter on Christmas, showcasing our favourite moments from recent Christmases, and you can bet your baked ham we had a vision board for every one of those themes. Without this, you won't get a gorgeous, cohesive look that stirs the emotions and puts a smile on your face.

We always say, 'Done is better than perfect', and we love this motto because it has the power to shake people out of a rut and make them take action with their home. If you're waiting for the perfect plan, the perfect timing and the perfect budget, you might be waiting for a very long time or you might miss the boat altogether.

If you aren't happy in your home, we want you to do SOMETHING – anything – to improve things and make progress. Another saying Lana loves is 'If you're not going forward, you're going backward'. We want you going forward, and we hope the tips and tricks in this book will help you to do exactly that. It's time to invest in your home. And 'invest' doesn't mean you need to throw a whole chunk of money at a reno (though you certainly can) so much as it means we want to encourage you to invest time, thought and effort into your home. The truth is that any home can be made to feel better, even on the tightest of budgets. It can be as simple as throwing a new bedsheet over a couch and styling it with new cushions, or you can go 'all in': knock the whole thing down and start from scratch. All that's required is a vision and a commitment to doing *something*.

Don't believe us? Maybe our bonus chapter will convince you. Showcasing stunning projects by a handful of our very own Reno School graduates, this chapter is proof that you don't need to be a Bird to create a beautiful home. These skills can be learned, and great things can happen when you have a clear vision and you take action. That's why we do what we do – to help you create your dream home, one step at a time.

We've got you, and you've got this!
Bonnie, Erin and Lana xxx

CHAPTER ONE

Colour me
HAMPTONS

FRESHER, BETTER, BRIGHTER

This is what you can achieve with a cosmetic reno.

Bubbling just under the surface of this typical double-storey plain Jane was a Cape Cod queen waiting to bust loose. It was up to us to coax her out of her shell. Her owners loved their neighbourhood and loved their home, but they needed a layout (and look) that would suit their family of five much better.

Thankfully, this brick home had a lot going for it: a big footprint on a great-sized block with a big, flat backyard featuring a swimming pool (albeit one that had seen better days). Our excited home owners handed over their keys, their budget and full creative control to us! We sent them on their merry way and sprang into action to give them that family home they'd been dreaming of. Their only requests were that we create open-plan living and update the house for modern life.

While we definitely made some structural changes, cosmetic changes did most of the heavy lifting on this job. It's proof that you really can revive a fading beauty with some make-up and fresh accessories.

BEFORE

AFTER

Who said you have to centre art?

#NOWAYMONET

Raise your side-table game with a sculptural piece.

BEFORE

HUE CUES

Stripes and blue tones were perfectly in line with our Hamptons theme, so we used both of those elements in this formal lounge room and throughout the house. Stripes are clean and modern, so adding a few floral cushions made things feel a bit more traditional. And even though the Moroccan-inspired pattern on the coffee table is miles away from the Hamptons, the colour works and its modern form and shape add some edge.

COLOUR IS KING WITH ART

Just because the theme of your house is one thing doesn't mean the art you choose can't go in another direction. Our vision said Hamptons, but we weren't keen on traditional paintings of coastlines and anchors. The piece we chose feels young and fresh. And it works because the colour palette is a match made in the Hamptons. Those blues and pops of gold in the art tie in perfectly with the colour palette of the room.

USE SHAPE TO BRING BALANCE

The day bed, the windows, the wall mouldings, the pillows ... there were a lot of rectangles and squares going on in this room. Bringing in rounded shapes in the form of the coffee table, wall sconces and homewares balanced these out a treat and made the room feel more harmonious.

15

"The minute we decided to put a built-in day bed under the feature window, I asked our builders to frame it up and hinge the seat so it could double as a sneaky storage spot. It doesn't cost much to make these changes, but you'll be glad that you spent the money when you're folding up blankets a few months down the track and you've got the perfect spot to store them. Start thinking about built-in seats, wall bump-outs and entrances to rooms as opportunities to add extra storage. It's such a simple and cost-effective way to keep your home looking beautiful and clutter-free for years to come."

Erin

STEAL STORAGE? IS THAT EVEN LEGAL?

We converted a gloomy under-stair cupboard in the entryway into this beautiful nook, and now this home makes a statement as soon as the front door is opened. A bench seat, wall sconce and some beautiful tiles make this a really special feature area. And don't worry, we haven't sacrificed storage completely – it's just tucked away, under the seat.

★ **DIY HACK** ★

Go potty!

It's hard to go wrong with large white pots. They look great with pretty much any style and colour of home, and they're really easy to create. DIY if you've got old terracotta pots. You can paint them up in a weekend to look just like this.

≪≪≪
AMP UP YOUR ENTRY

1 **Freshen it up with fancy flooring.** We carried these encaustic-look tiles from the front porch right through the entry to create a seamless transition and a bit of a 'moment'. If you're working with floorboards, you could jazz things up by laying the boards in a herringbone or chevron pattern in the entry.

2 **Make it brighter.** Entering someone's home should be an uplifting experience. If your entry suffers from a lack of light, then crisp white paint and glass panels in the front door will go a long way to brightening things up. Vertical cladding can also create texture and the illusion of higher ceilings.

3 **Add a seat.** Bench seats are a winner in every room of the home, but we especially love having one by the front door. Who doesn't find it more comfortable to perch while taking off their shoes? If you don't have a suitable nook, or if a built-in isn't in your budget, then a freestanding bench seat also does the trick. #Lanasgoldenrule

4 **Style it up.** Pots, plants, hooks and pretty prints all have a place in a front entry. The trick is to remember that less is more. Don't overcrowd the space.

DON'T DITCH THE ARCH

How many older homes have these arches? LOADS! But before you swing the sledgehammer, ask yourself if you could make a feature out of that curved creation. We clad this side of the wall and sprayed the brick on the other. Now, whichever way we look at it, we love the archway. It creates a peek-a-boo portal into the room beyond – making the whole scene a piece of art in itself.

This was a cosmetic makeover only – no structural changes were made here.

BEFORE

AFTER

<<<

Surround
bold art with
whites and
neutrals to
make it a
focal point.

WONDER WALL

That's what we call this wall of little windows. It was a load-bearing wall that we couldn't remove during the reno due to time and money constraints ... but we desperately wanted to create a visual connection between the kitchen and lounge room. *Voilà!* Could a 'wonder wall' be the answer to your open-plan ambitions?

Unreal!

This pretty pot plant is pretty unreal, isn't it? Yep, it's 100 per cent fake, which means it looks this good all the time.

Feature wall?
Nah, we prefer
a feature ceiling!

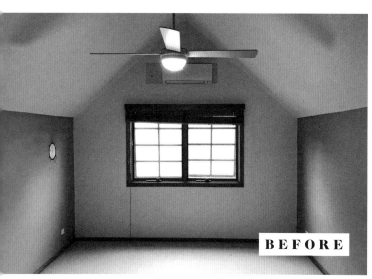

BEFORE

COLOUR FLIP

Flipping a colour scheme on its head can create the illusion of a wider space in a room that is tall and a bit skinny. How easy is that?

THE GOOD KIND OF CAVITY

A major space-saving move in this room was placing the double bed in the wall cavity. If you have a wall cavity, lucky you! This is precious real estate.

Wallpaper inside
the cavity gives
this bed nook
a designer feel.

Added crosshatch details keep it classic Hamptons.

Safari vibes

IN THE PINK

What little lady wouldn't fall head over heels for a bedroom with her very own built-in bunk painted in the softest pink – Dulux 'Lipgloss', to be precise.

NO DRAGGING MATTRESSES INTO THIS ROOM

The beauty of a bed design like this is that it provides plenty of opportunity for play when they're little, and it's ready to go when the sleepovers start. Being able to sleep three to a room is a godsend. (Lana says she'd give anything to have this in her 13-year-old's room right now!)

Hot tip

Bi-fold shutter doors are a great substitute for a wall when you don't want to close off a flexi-room permanently. And if those bi-folds happen to be white shutters like these, then they play an even bigger role because they bring their special beachy quality to the party. Open the doors, and you've got a light and airy common area. Close them, and you've got a private sanctuary. It's all about options!

Whimsical wallpaper says 'this is a powder room'.

What type of skirt? You can choose standard skirting boards or continue the floor tile 10 cm up the wall.

THE POWDER ROOM/ LAUNDRY CAN BE A SMART COMPROMISE

When you're renovating, one of the things you learn pretty quick is that you can't have it all (#funpolice). That's why we often choose to combine our laundry and powder room into one. Both are considered wet rooms, and each requires plumbing, so, if you're short on space, this approach makes perfect sense to us.

FANCY A FRONT-LOADER?

We're big fans of front-loaders, because you can slide them under a bench or stack them like this using a stacking kit. Stacking without one can be dangerous and damage your appliances. You want them to stack securely (think Lego rather than Jenga). If you can, look for one that offers extra features. Some have sliding shelves that come in handy when space is tight and you want to fold clothes or need a ledge for detergent.

SQUARE BATHROOMS CAN WORK, TOO

Our ideal bathroom layout is one where the toilet is hidden from view, the freestanding bath is the hero, there's a separate walk-in shower and, of course, a gorgeous vanity. It's much easier to fit all of this in a long, skinny bathroom than a chubby, square one – but that's what we got here. That's why we resorted to this shower-over-bath setup. It's never our first choice, but don't throw the (design) towel in if that's what you're dealing with – it can still be pretty and it's a real space saver if a bathtub is a must.

Think of pretty hooks and fluffy white towels as art for your bathroom walls. We do!

LOVE AT FIRST SIGHT

What do you see first when you walk into your bathroom? Whatever it is (hopefully not the toilet, gulp), THAT thing needs to be the hero. In this case, it was the wall behind the bathtub/shower. Gorgeous encaustic-look tiles and fancypants tapware make for a stunning first impression.

THE RIGHT BATH FOR THE JOB

Finding a bathtub that can moonlight as a shower isn't easy. It needs to have a near-vertical surface up the end where you want to stand so that you can get your feet right in under the shower head. This nifty little tub also slopes gently at the end under the window, if you want to lean back.

GOOD NEWS FOR BORING BEDROOMS EVERYWHERE

If you've got a bland bedroom crying out for some style, sass and sophistication – you CAN cosmetically transform it so that it becomes unrecognisable. In this room, we added:

★ panelling to walls
★ fresh paint
★ new shutters
★ new carpet
★ new bedhead
★ new bed linens.

Et voilà! Transformed.

CREATE A CLEAN CANVAS

White bed linen, furniture and wall colour make a great blank canvas and can help prevent a room from feeling fussy or overdone. Even the marble shell on the bedside table is quite minimalist. Here, the white base colour allows the beautiful blue bedhead and patterned cushions to make a statement.

NEW GEN CARPETS

Updating a daggy carpet can work wonders for a bedroom. And the latest and greatest carpets have levels of stain, soil, wear and colourfast performance that blow us away. This one is made from a new premium fibre called eco+ triexta, which is made with 37% polymer from corn sugar of all things! It's hard-wearing, stain resistant and has a soft, luxurious texture your toes will adore. We chose a pretty light colour in this low-traffic, kid-free zone. It's pale and plush and just lovely.

The gold candelabra is the one quirk in this room.

LOW + MEDIUM + HIGH

It doesn't take much to pretty up a bedside table. All you need is a few simple items of varying heights. Here, we've used a flat dish (low), candle (medium) and vase of flowers (high) to create a stylish mini moment. And there's still room for a good book and a cup of tea.

VISION-WORTHY HARDWARE

We set our sights firmly on the Hamptons, and with that as our destination, chrome tapware and cup handles were the only way to go. They stay true to that traditional aesthetic and work beautifully with the blues and whites in the room. We love gold and brass finishes, but they wouldn't have brought the Hamptons vision to life as effectively.

SWAP THE DOOR

These bi-fold shutters give the feeling of more space in this ensuite. We actually used the same polysatin shutters as we did on the windows, just taller!

POWER POINTS: LOVE AND LOATHE THEM

Pop your power points on the side of your vanity (the side not facing the doorway) if possible. That way they're still really accessible but they won't muck up the aesthetic of the tiling above the vanity.

True to form

It wouldn't have been a true Hamptons kitchen without
a ceramic butler's sink and classic chrome mixer.

DOUBLE CHUNK

A skinny benchtop wouldn't have looked right on top of
these chunky legs, but this 100 mm thick stone benchtop
balances them out perfectly. Always choose your stone and
cabinetry together – that's what we call a 'handcuff decision'.

PENDANT PERFECTION

These babies are hung at juuuust the right height in this
kitchen – we recommend anywhere between 700–850 mm
from benchtop to base of pendant.

MAXIMISE DINING TIME

Running a bench seat along the back of the dining nook was
key to making the space look larger. This bench is 2.8 metres
long and can fit a fair few kids along it.

MATCH YOUR CROSSHATCH

Look for furniture that lives in the same world as the one
you're creating. The backs of the dining chairs pick up on
the crosshatch details in the kitchen, tying both spaces
together beautifully.

REPEAT THE TILE

Tiling at the back of your house can make the area feel that bit more special while also creating that 'outdoor room' feeling. If you've used tiles at the front of your house, repeating that same pattern at the back will create a sense of flow and cohesion.

OUTDOOR SHUTTERS

Did you know that you can use shutters outside, too? True story! Not only do they do a great job of controlling the light and ventilation in this outdoor room, they also look *fab-u-lous* and, even better, they block out the neighbours.

STYLE WITH SPECIAL OCCASIONS IN MIND

Outdoor dining areas are casual by nature, but they can rise to the occasion when necessary. We mixed gorgeous wicker armchairs with a bench seat (we love doing this) to elevate the look of this outdoor table. Now it's a superb space for casual barbecues, and it can easily be fancied up for special meals such as an alfresco Christmas lunch (see pages 204–5 for some great tips).

WEATHER-RESISTANT WICKER?

It's really a thing! Even though these beautiful chairs are undercover, we still wanted to use outdoor furniture that could go the distance.

DETAILS, DETAILS

The theme continues with the crosshatch details on those crisp white glass cabinets. These make the style of this kitchen clear and add a homey and inviting feeling.

REMEMBER YOUR ROOF TILES

Imagine if this roof tile was a terracotta colour! The moment would look and feel completely different. Now the roof has been replaced, it looks as pretty as the new kitchen – and who would have thought that was possible?

Gardening never looked so good!

#NOZZLEENVY

Two words: outdoor room.

(If you say you don't want
one, we won't believe you.)

BEFORE

MAXIMISE THE OUTDOORS BY ZONING FOR LIFE

Designing an outdoor area that you'll fall in love with is all about zoning. Ideally, you want an area to lounge and somewhere to eat – but if you're short on outdoor space, choose the zone that's most important to you and create that. We created six zones (yes, SIX!) in this back garden:

1 Outdoor kitchen and bar
2 Dining area
3 Lounging/day bed
4 Pool
5 Fire pit
6 Mini basketball court.

Hot tip

Even if you don't have a big backyard, try sketching up a few distinct spaces that work for the way you and your family like to live outdoors. This is always a great starting point when designing your landscaping.

From bitsy to big

Older houses that have had second-storey additions or extensions built some decades ago can end up looking like a patchwork quilt. Painting this two-tone exterior one consistent colour instantly made the house look bigger and more cohesive. Boom!

Swap the fire pit for an
outdoor coffee table when the
weather heats up, and winter's
'roasting marshmallows' moment
becomes summer's 'tapas and
tonic' time. Viva flexibility!

DON'T UNDERESTIMATE THE POWER OF OUTDOOR CUSHIONS

Not only do they make any outdoor space feel 'like home', but also if you pick the right patterns and colours then your vision board literally comes to life. #hellohamptons! Don't be afraid to judge that cushion by its cover.

MODULAR WALL

What a difference a modular wall makes! Can you imagine how this space would look without it? They look great, provide an enormous amount of privacy and also create an acoustic barrier. #theneighbourswillloveyou! Modular walls are pre-fabricated sheets on piers. They have the look of a rendered brick wall, but cost a whole lot less in materials and labour. And the best part: they show up on site in sections that are ready to go. Your builders can erect them in no time flat and all it takes to make them look amazing is a lick of pretty exterior paint.

CHAPTER TWO

Mediterranean
FARMHOUSE

CLUB MED MEETS THE HINTERLAND

Many moons ago, Sophie Bell (aka Peppa Hart) joined the Three Birds family as our website designer/digital guru. Four years later, Sophie – who we were referring to as the 'fourth bird' by this point – dropped the amazing news that she and her hubby had just purchased their dream block of land just 30 minutes from Byron Bay in the hinterland.

Our hearts and minds simultaneously exploded as we all saw this moment for what it was: a once-in-a-lifetime opportunity to work together and build a truly special home from the ground up that combined minimalist style with maximum wow factor.

This collab was a massive undertaking, and it became a labour of love for all of us. Together, we brought Soph's dream of a Mediterranean farmhouse to life in this idyllic corner of the bush.

When we broke ground on the block, the Bells were a family of three. By the time the last cushion was fluffed, they were a family of four with a stunning home purpose-built for family life and entertaining. We've created the ultimate hinterland hideaway – a place where their friends and family can gather, stay and enjoy all the best things about our outdoor Aussie lifestyle. It's their own slice of paradise, and they couldn't be happier.

From sea to tree

#HIDEAWAYWITHME

BEFORE

AFTER

THE MANY PROS OF BUILDING NEW

1 **Better insulation:** Many older homes built around the postwar years are solid, but their insulation leaves a lot to be desired. In fact, if they are insulated at all, it's often with newspaper (no joke, we've seen it!). When you build new, you know exactly what's behind your walls, and you can feel confident that it's going to do the job.

2 **Airtight windows:** If an older home has beautiful timber windows, chances are it will also have some gaps around those windows – gaps that are letting cold air in and hot air out during winter. #moneyoutthewindow! Installing new windows gives you peace of mind that things are exactly as they should be.

3 **A more comfortable home:** Today's building regulations encompass things such as energy star ratings, thermal efficiency and solar aspects. All of these things contribute to a more comfortable home.

4 **Better technology in the building materials:** The latest in building materials means that the end result is a house that is cheaper to heat and cool, and is therefore more energy efficient.

5 **More flexibility when it comes to design:** In a new home, you have the real luxury of positioning the footprint, windows and doors to suit the orientation of the site, making the most of the sunshine, views and breezes.

6 **Easier to maintain:** New building materials tend to require far less maintenance and upkeep than traditional ones.

7 **Less susceptible to termites:** Framing materials are now pre-treated to be termite resistant *before* they even get to your building site. And the less chance those critters have to eat you out of house and home, the better.

8 **Building new can be cheaper than a reno:** Pulling a house apart during a renovation can reveal nasty – and sometimes expensive – surprises, such as cracked foundations, old wiring, and crumbling brick walls. #beenthere!

"I had visualised and hand-drawn exactly how we wanted the house to look, and this image is almost identical to that sketch. The steps blending into the grass, the trees enveloping the house, the white textured walls and curves … it's all a dream come to life."

— Sophie Bell

Is there a fresher colour combo than green and white?

SET THE TONE

The entryway is the perfect place to showcase the inspiration behind your home. If guests aren't clued in to the style of it by the time they're at your front door, then they will be the minute they step inside. Here, those arched doors swing open to reveal white walls, clean lines, oversized prints of Mediterranean beach life and beautifully sculptural urns. There's no doubt that this is a slice of the Med come to life in Australia.

WE LOVE A NON-KITCHEN-Y KITCHEN

Open-plan layouts show no sign of falling out of fashion anytime soon, and that's because they transcend style and trends; they're a lifestyle choice. If you're going open-plan with your layout, chances are your kitchen will be on display 24/7. Sophie wanted hers to look 'more like an entertaining space than a kitchen'. We achieved that by:

- ⭐ tucking the fridge out of sight (more on that in a minute)
- ⭐ keeping all of the cabinetry *below* the benchtops
- ⭐ installing beautiful windows along the back wall rather than a more traditional stone or tiled splashback.

That simplicity, combined with the pared back decorative touches, makes this an area that feels light, inviting and completely in step with the rest of the large, open-plan living space.

A SLEEK, SEAMLESS ISLAND

There's no doubt that the hero in this kitchen is that huge island. We often say that things are seamless, but this island literally is. If you love a seamless look (i.e. no joins in sight), then a concrete benchtop might be for you. It can be poured on site so it dries into one glorious piece – like a sculpture. How good is that?

ADD A SUPER-SPESH PENDANT

In case you're wondering, we don't hang pendants in our kitchens for extra light. These babies fall into what we like to call the 'Just Looks Hot' category. That's where a light is installed because the fitting itself is so beautiful. Pendants help to make a kitchen look and feel more special than just a place to wash dishes and pack lunches. Your lighting-style inspo should jump right off your vision board. You can also look at your handles and tapware for a tip-off.

Here's a tip when you're hanging a pendant light ... if you don't get it exactly where you want it on the ceiling, have your sparky lengthen the wire and then attach it to a hook that is in the perfect spot. #lookscutetoo

Island paradise!

LET'S TALK CONCRETE

Concrete enthusiasts love it for its raw aesthetic, which suits an industrial, organic or minimalist look. While it's great for many purposes, it does have a few drawbacks in the kitchen:

1   It's prone to chipping, because the edges can be quite brittle.

2   Concrete, much like marble, is porous, which means that it will absorb liquids and can stain in sections where the sealant has worn off.

3   It doesn't fare well when hot pans make contact with the surface, as the sealant will discolour. Trivets to put those hot pots and pans down on are a must.

4   It requires resealing to protect it from wear and tear, and to keep it looking its rustic best.

5   It's not cheap! The cost is similar to engineered stone and even some types of marble.

Concrete is unique. So if you've got your heart set on it and you're going into the purchase with your eyes open, then go for it and love it for the quirky, delicate and high-maintenance material it is.

Hot tip

If you love the concrete look but want something more low maintenance, then engineered stone (aka quartz) is a good option. You can find it in a range of finishes that have a concrete look, but with the durability of quartz. #winwin!

DON'T SCRIMP ON THE SPLASHBACK VIEW

With all the light and green that a window splashback lets into a kitchen, it's easy to see why they're becoming more popular. But if you're going down this road, keep in mind that you'll need to give that garden lots of TLC to keep it looking feature-worthy. And don't forget to add external lights, or it will look spectacular during the day but like a black hole at night.

YOU DON'T HAVE TO PUT THE FRIDGE ON SHOW

Placing the fridge in the butler's pantry was a controversial decision, but having it in the main kitchen would have compromised our vision of a 'non-kitchen-y kitchen'. A few years down the track, Soph confirms that this set-up still totally works for her.

If you're going to put your fridge in the butler's pantry, locate it just inside the entryway, so it's only an arm's length away from the main kitchen.

Love these rattan handles!

LIVEN UP WHITE WALLS

When you've got a lot of white walls, a great way to add texture and interest is by enhancing existing architectural details or including new ones, such as these arched niches that we strategically placed throughout this home. They are a nod to the organic rendered forms you see everywhere in Greece – adding that sprinkle of Med magic – while they also provide a place to display sculptural pieces.

BRING ON BREAKFAST

We love a breakfast nook. Even if the dining table isn't far away, nooks near the kitchen are super handy for snatching a morning moment of Zen over a coffee and a newspaper. They also make the perfect 'kids' table' when you've got other families over. Kids love having their own adult-free space in which to socialise, and adults usually enjoy the separation, too!

TONE ON TONE

The bronzed bods in the large print look like they're straight off an Ibiza beach, which not only suits this modern Mediterranean farmhouse theme but also matches the colour palette – the tones are perfectly in step with this space. Jackpot!

When hanging multiple pendants, aim to leave 650–750 mm between them so they don't look too crowded.

TRUE OR FALSE: YOUR TIMBERS NEED TO MATCH

False! You can totally mix your timbers and end up with something that looks ... *chef's kiss*. In fact, we love that there are many different shades of timber in this house. The different tones bring a lot of warmth and are one of our favourite features.

SUNDAY LUNCHES HERE, PLEASE

The size of the dining table you choose will depend on how many mouths you typically feed and how large or small the space is that you are styling. Since we had a huge open-plan space to work with, we chose a dining table that was big enough to seat at least eight people. You may have noticed that we love mixing a bench seat in with our dining chairs. We like the way it looks, but it also means that you can squeeze in lots more bums – especially if they're little ones. This is the perfect set-up for dinner parties and lazy weekend lunches with friends. In fact, Sophie tells us that this solid timber table is her number one fave piece of furniture in the house.

AN OFFICE YOU NEVER WANT TO LEAVE

Plenty of natural light, fresh air and open space make this the home office of our dreams. That large table is perfect for meetings, and the long runs of flat-pack IKEA cabinetry along the walls keep things organised, tidy *and* stylish.

This room just wouldn't feel the same without this arched window.

DEADSET STYLISH

Who would have thought that a dead palm frond would be a styling 'yes'? This one totally works in this space, because it brings height and interest to the otherwise bare corner of the room. It also bridges the gap between those lush green palms in the print (and just outside the window) and the pinky brown tones of the room.

Special touches such as the Slim Aarons print and the custom bedhead (painted by Sophie's mum) make this a guestroom any of us would feel at home in.

Is this the mother of all modulars?

SUPERSIZE THAT SOFA

One of the first things you might notice in this room is that we have out sofa-ed all our other houses with this one, the mother of all modulars. If you've got a large living space, a modular sofa can be a great way to get the look of a huge custom couch *without* breaking the bank. Ka-ching! We created this one using eight modules – it's pretty much a giant Tetris – and its beauty is in its flexibility. No matter what you feel like doing or which way you want to face, there's a spot on this gorgeous sofa for you.

BORN TO PARTY

This house is an entertainer's dream. If guests are in your future, then it pays to maximise seating. We provided loads of seating options in this space – can you spy 18 spots? In addition to the dining chairs and sofa, there's a comfy armchair, a few floor cushions and a concrete bench seat that doubles as a mantelpiece. But that's not all! Take a look *juuuust* outside on the verandah, and you'll spot two more seats – and you can swing from those ones!

Floor cushions instantly relax a space.

FAMILY-FRIENDLY TIMBER

We chose engineered timber for the flooring throughout this home, not only for its good looks, but also for the way it *feels* underfoot. A bonus is that it's so damn easy to clean. Despite dogs, kids, spills, pizza parties and guests galore wandering about in stilettos and muddy shoes, it comes up good every time. Soph tells us that she just whips out her trusty vacuum, gives it a once-over, and it's like new. She's also noticed that the subtle grain in the timber is great for helping her disguise a bit of mess in between cleans.

"Okay, let's address the elephant in the room: that all-white couch. I get asked about my white couches all the time, because I've got four boys, dogs and – let's face it – adults in my house. But I've long believed that white is easier to maintain than other colours, and here's why: I go for sofa covers that can be spot-cleaned with baby wipes and washed. When accidents happen, I jump on them quick smart to minimise the damage. Slip covers and Napisan are your best friends, and if you know that you've got a load of kids coming over, then a white sheet thrown over the couch isn't a bad idea, either."

Bonnie

Make mine a double

(BARN DOOR, THAT IS).

QUIET PLEASE

A second living space is a must in most family homes, but quite often the two living spaces end up being near each other. That's when adding glass doors such as these barn-door sliders can be a good move. They keep things light and open, but limit the noise transfer from one space to another – especially if you use noise-reducing glass!

What's better than one hanging chair? Two!

ROUGH-INS AREN'T JUST FOR THE INTERIOR

Your builder and electrician will need to prepare the ceiling cavity and rough-in the electricals early in the build process – not only inside the home, but also outside. If you are planning covered porches and outdoor rooms like this one, make ALL of your lighting decisions (inside and out) nice and early. That way, you won't reach the styling stage and realise that your special outdoor area will have to be lit by candlelight or iPhone torches. #planningfail

STATEMENT PENDANT OUTSIDE?

You bet! The covered portico ensures that this pendant and anyone sitting under it stay dry and beautiful, no matter what the weather is doing. And the fact that it matches the pendant in the kitchen adds to the sense that this outdoor room is a continuation of what's going on inside the house. It provides a touch of drama and sophistication, and creates a major mood in this outdoor room.

WINDOWS ARE A GREAT INVESTMENT

You only need to look at this laundry to understand what a BIG impact windows can have on the interior of a home. After all, few things look and feel better in a house than natural light. Even so, windows can often slip down the list of priorities during a renovation or build, when it's easy to get distracted by more glamorous decisions involving kitchens and fancypants furniture. But please don't cut corners when choosing your windows and deciding where they're going to go – you'll end up kicking yourself later when your house feels dark and gloomy rather than light and breezy.

YOU SPIN ME RIGHT ROUND

'Shape' is one of the key elements of design, and it's something we think about a lot when designing a room. Naturally, the round window is the star in this laundry, but the handles on the cabinets and tapware got the circular memo, too – even the laundry appliances came to the party! It's not often that appliances *enhance* the style score of a laundry. #sexycircles

Easy access to the clothes line is your friend in a laundry room.

Hot tip

FRONT-LOADERS ARE BECOMING THE FRONT-RUNNERS

It's true! Front-loading washing machines are starting to outsell their top-loading equivalents in many parts of the world, and for good reason. Not only do they provide more bench space (always a bonus), but they are also gentler on clothes, use less water and less detergent than top-loaders, *and* they cost less to run. That's a lot of pros. The compromise is that they can come with a higher price tag and their cycles generally take longer (unless you choose a quick wash). Newer models even have an 'add sock' function, which allows you to add items after the cycle has started – something you only used to be able to do with a top-loader. As if that wasn't enough to seal their top spot, front-loaders look so much nicer, especially when they're next to a matching dryer. We're sold!

This is one of our favourite windows in the house!

We love these custom louvre cupboards, and they're perfect for ventilation in a laundry room.

Marrakesh render

NICHE NEEDS

Shower niches come in all shapes and sizes, and the size of yours will depend on personal preference. A good guide is around 300 mm high – that's tall enough to accommodate those shampoo value packs – 100 mm deep and as wide as you please.

BATHED IN LIGHT

It's so important to think about where the sun will be at different times of the day and how you can bring that natural light inside – either with windows (such as these big, beautiful bi-folds) or with doors and skylights. This is especially true in bathrooms, because putting make-up on in actual daylight is the gold standard. No blending mishaps here!

FIXATE ON FIXTURES ASAP

If there's a bathroom reno in your future, then we recommend that you go virtual-shopping the minute you know in which direction your vision board is pointing. The earlier in the planning process you go, the better. We had these fixtures and fittings earmarked before we'd even confirmed the bathroom layouts!

CONFIRM THOSE COSTS

While you're browsing fixtures and fittings, save the price of each product on your phone so you can add those costs to your budget spreadsheet later (if you don't have a budget spreadsheet, then you need one). Failing to eyeball items and prices could mean that you end up with a bathroom bill bigger than your budget. #ouch

Hot tip

DISCOVER LIVING BRASS

The fixtures we chose for this house have a rare quality that we love in a product: they get better with age! This 'living brass' will develop a gorgeous patina over time as it gets used and touched, making it perfectly imperfect.

Big bi-folds =
open-air bathing

Check out these gorgeous handpainted crosses on the arch.

A BUILT-IN BED

In a parents' retreat this spacious, the bed has to hold its own. It should be large enough so that the scale of it makes sense with the proportion of the room, but finding one that is the right size and shape can be costly. So what do you do when you can't find the perfect bed? Well, if you're uber-handy, like Soph's hubby, you build it! He framed up the bed in timber, sheeted it with blue board and then rendered it. And he didn't stop at the bed: he built side tables, too. Definitely NOT the simplest of tasks, but what a beautiful job he did. Now that's a handy hubby!

A CLEAN WHITE BEDHEAD CAN CREATE CONTRAST

We decided to make this bedhead a white-out to allow those striking Mediterranean vibes to come through and to provide a strong contrast to the rich colour of the linens. There was already enough drama going on in this room thanks to the architectural details and the view outside – painting the large bedhead a particular colour would have pulled focus from those features.

Talk about an epic main bedroom!

Can you
believe it's from
IKEA?

"Our walk-in robe was such a big space that the estimate for getting custom joinery fitted was not far off the cost for fitting an entire kitchen. (Pass the paper bag, we're hyperventilating!) If you've ever been quoted for custom joinery before, then you'll know that it can be a real budget buster. That's when I knew that I needed to look at other options for our wardrobes and office storage. We'd used the PAX wardrobe system in a previous reno and loved it, so off to IKEA I went. I love an organised wardrobe; all those felt jewellery drawers and sunglasses drawers are right up my alley!"

– Sophie Bell

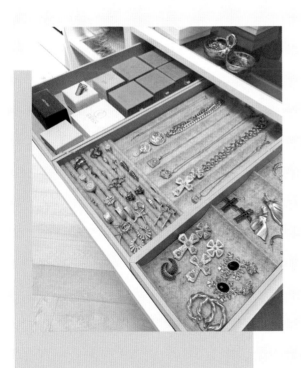

WONDERFUL WARDROBES

Like most IKEA products, Sophie's wardrobes arrived as flat packs. It was daunting for her to see 4 TONNES of cabinets on the driveway, so she was super relieved that she'd paid the extra fee for IKEA to build the wardrobes on site. She's sure her husband would have left her if she'd delegated that job to him. His list was long enough!

'Now that the wardrobes are in and we're using them every day, I can honestly say that they're fabulous, both in looks and functionality,' Sophie says. 'I can't fault any of the products we chose. My one piece of advice would be that just because you're not using "custom" products, it doesn't mean that you can't make them look custom. You'd never guess that these cupboards weren't purpose-built for the space – they even soft close.'

Notice how this vanity ties back to the kitchen joinery? Even the handles are the same. Repetition in design is a great way to make a home feel cohesive.

Change it up

Customise your child's furniture to suit the colour scheme of their room. This little IKEA table took no time to spray paint, and it looks extra adorable now.

Recess the blinds inside picture windows to keep those lines crisp and clean.

PRINTS CAN
BE PERSONAL

Family portraits can be #awkward, but they
don't have to be. Turn your favourite family
candids into statement prints, and then use
them throughout your home to make it truly
yours. This oh-so-cute baby bum belongs to
Sophie's son, Hendrix, making this a one-of-
a-kind print full of sentimental meaning.

DETAILS ARE WORTH GETTING RIGHT

Most people would have slapped a glass balustrade on this balcony without a second thought, but our vision board told us that this wasn't the best choice. To stay true to that vision of a Mediterranean farmhouse, we needed a more authentic take on a balustrade. This amazing handmade balustrade was sourced from a local supplier, and it gives the upper-level verandah (and the whole back of the house, if we're honest) that Med feeling we were all chasing. Mission accomplished!

RENDER WITH BENEFITS

We used a high-density polystyrene called NRG Greenboard for this build. It's a totally new way to achieve a rendered look WITHOUT the hefty cost of laying bricks and mortar first. It's lightweight and cost effective, and because it contains fire retardant, it's suitable for use in bushfire-prone areas. It even contains vermin retardant! What will they think of next? One of its biggest benefits is that it provides awesome insulation, which is so important when building an energy-efficient home. And from a looks point of view, we especially love this material because it can easily be shaped to create the enviable arches that were so integral to the design of this house. Once it's all in place, it gets rendered and painted. The result is a seamless finish with many hidden benefits.

SHOWER UNDER THE STARS

If you want that holiday feeling at home, be inspired by your favourite vacation spots. We took our inspo from those villa bathrooms in Bali where you step outside to shower. This family only has a few peeping-Tom koalas to worry about, so it was too good an opportunity to pass up.

> "Waking up to the view of the rainforest every morning and showering on the terrace is all our favourite hotels rolled into one dream bedroom. I still wake up every morning and cannot believe it's real."
>
> – SOPHIE BELL

Hot tip

Concrete pavers are a must if you want to protect your lawn from constant foot traffic. These cute-as-a-button pavers continue our round theme while also providing a clear path to tiptoe over to the pool. Who says big square pavers are the only way to go?

White + green + rattan =
holiday!

HOW TO NAIL THAT OUTDOOR ROOM FEELING »»»

1 Mirror the materials and colours used for the main house. By rendering the benchtop and creating an arch along the back of the pavilion, we've tied it in with the look of the main house. We also incorporated the same v-groove cladding and quirky tiles.

2 Light it as if it were an indoor space. The large pendant above the dining table and the outdoor sconces look gorgeous and also create a warm, homey glow once the sun goes down.

3 Plan the flow as carefully as you would an indoor space. Think about how people will use the space, especially if you've got a few zones. You want to provide enough room for people to sit, stand and move around comfortably.

BRING THE BEACH CLUB HOME

Ahhh, day beds. Bringing the Bali beach-club vibes to pool areas since ... forever! Day beds are the ultimate for relaxing with a book, supervising swimmers in the pool or lounging the summer days away. This double day bed measures 3 x 3 metres – large enough for a few bodies to lounge, snuggle or snooze in style.

FREE-RANGE BAR

A bar cart or drinks trolley not only gives you extra storage, but it also looks divine and brings a relaxed holiday vibe to any home. #yeswayrosé! Stock it with some good-looking glassware, a few bottles of your best plus some lemons and limes. Just watch out for roaming toddlers who may want to take it for a walk.

ENTERTAINER'S PARADISE

Family life revolves around the home, so if you can, why not create an outdoor area that brings the party to you? If your slice of alfresco heaven is going to be set back from your house, as this one is, it pays to hook it up to water and electricity so you and your guests have all the lights, fridges and sinks you need to live it up late into the evening. The only thing you'll need to run inside for is the bathroom. #naturecalls

CHAPTER THREE

The bold
EXTENSION

FROM BEIGE TO BOMBSHELL

Which change do you think made the biggest difference?

For this project, we went back to our roots and did one of our trademark quickie renos of a typical suburban Aussie eyesore. And boy, was this 1960s house ripe for a reno. It ticked all of the boxes for us: at face value, the poor thing had very few endearing features, was lacking character and had absolutely no street appeal. We knew this ugly duckling had the potential to become a beautiful swan.

Thankfully, the small house was on a good-sized block. By blowing out the back of the house and adding an extension, we increased the footprint by 70 square metres. We also moved some internal walls around to improve the flow and functionality inside *and* outside.

Fast-forward 12 weeks, and this beige babe was ready for her comeback. Two black and white awnings were the finishing touch, just like a pair of false eyelashes – the minute those went on, the house came to life. Now she's glam and gorgeous, with entertaining space to spare and enough charm to make the neighbours stop and stare ... in a good way.

BEFORE

AFTER

GIVE THE FACADE A FACELIFT

Be on the lookout for ways to add beauty to your home's facade and also make it a spot you'll actually spend time in. Adding a verandah to the front of this house brought dimension to the formerly flat frontage and another spot to relax and let the world go by.

PRIVACY SCREENS CHANGE EVERYTHING

Our love of privacy screens runs deep, and here's why: these simple screens are easy to construct, but they have the power to turn dead space into an area you'll use all the time. This screen looks great *and* blocks the view of the car park next door (yep, it's there, you just can't see it!). What was once dead space is now the perfect spot for a sundowner.

LINES FOR DAYS

Notice how we've used lines as a styling element in this outdoor area? Bold stripes show up on the pillows and the statement awnings, but the architectural elements – the privacy screen, decking, balustrade and doors – also feature lines. Horizontal lines (such as those created by the cladding) help spaces to feel more relaxed and casual, while vertical lines work well when you want something to feel that little bit more posh.

Concrete tiles age like fine wine – they literally get stronger over time.

DIY HACK

⋘ *Shell yeah!*

Giant clamshells look *ah*-mazing, can be styled a million ways and bring a natural touch to any setting – especially if you decide to fill them to the brim with soil and pretty succulents. These giant shells are artificial (made from resin), so they're visually stunning, durable *and* available in lots of different sizes.

DEEPER BLACKS ON DETAILS ADD DEPTH

Believe it or not, choosing the right shade of black can be just as hard as choosing a white paint. If you're tempted over to the dark side, then using a deeper shade of black for architectural accents such as doors and trims will create dimension and depth. We used Dulux 'Domino' on the house, and the deeper, purer 'Black' on the French doors. Can you spot the difference?

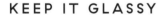

THE CLASSIC CABINET CONUNDRUM

We are often asked about how to finish kitchen cabinetry in a room with a raked ceiling. In this room, we've taken the cabinets up to the height where the rake begins, no bulkhead required.

CREATE SPACES THAT PLAY WELL WITH EACH OTHER

If we'd gone bold with colour and pattern in this seating area, then the statement kitchen next door to it would have been fighting for attention. Keeping things neutral creates a calming feel, while bringing in a mix of rich textures and metallic accents gives this area its own special feeling, so it isn't playing second fiddle to the kitchen.

KEEP IT GLASSY

A black and glass display cupboard is a great way to raise your kitchen game, but ONLY if you make a promise to yourself that it will be used to showcase pretty things. Chipped mugs and plastic kiddie cups need not apply.

SAME, SAME BUT ... SAME

If a white kitchen is calling your name, match the white paint on your cabinetry to the white on your walls and ceiling. It looks seamless because you avoid highlighting the subtle undertones of the different whites.

Crisp whites, blacks and neutrals allow a feature colour to step into the spotlight.

You don't need
real rafters to get this
look. Stick some faux
ones on, like we did.

#EASYPEASY

Tucking most of your appliances in the island will allow the cabinetry and other design features in the kitchen to shine. Putting ovens and microwaves along the back wall of this kitchen would have completely changed the aesthetic.

DON'T BE SCARED TO MIX UP STYLES

- ★ Apron sink = traditional
- ★ Black tapware = modern
- ★ Cabinet profile = traditional
- ★ Gold knobs = modern

KEEN ON GREEN?

There's so much to love about the colour green: it looks amazing; it comes in so many shades, from light-as-a-feather mint to bold emerald; it's a nod to nature; and it freshens up any room. If green is in your reno dreams, then you're in for a treat. And if you're afraid to make a bold statement, then muted, earthy greens can also be a great option. Just remember, the secret to creating a colourful kitchen that will stand the test of time is not to overdo it on colour. That's why we've limited the bold green hue to the island only.

CULTIVATE YOUR CURVES

With its soft curved ends and gorgeous colour, this island steals everyone's heart. Curves on a kitchen island are unexpected, so they add a subtle quirkiness to the room while also doing a great job of softening all of the hard corners and surfaces around them.

A 60 mm benchtop was calling our name in this kitchen.

FIND A VIEW AND THEN FRAME IT

Putting this huge window in the extension turned the hedge running along the back of the house into a beautiful feature. Now you can see green from just about anywhere in the main living areas.

CREATE A CAFÉ MOMENT

There's no rule that says you have to put a dining table right next to the kitchen (seriously, we checked!). By putting the dining table in the adjoining room, we were able to turn this area into an ideal spot to share a drink and some conversation.

We loved this statement chandelier so much that we used a super-sized version in another one of our homes. Check out page 171.

"The acoustic report for this house meant that this big window in the extension had to be made from noise-reducing glass due to nearby traffic noise. Luckily, we'd been down that busy road before. We added special glass (laminated acoustic glass, to be exact) to our budget and steamed ahead. Yes, it is more expensive than regular glass, but it reduces noise and has the added benefit of UV protection, which is good for your family and your furniture."

Lana

Rattan has the power to relax any room.

*White paint
makes a view pop!*

How plush is
this pooch's bed?
Lucky pup!

*Save $$$ in your WIR by hanging
curtains rather than cupboard doors.*

OOH LA LIGHT!

If you've found some outdoor lights that are just too pretty to leave outside, don't! We love these outdoor carriage lights in this main bedroom – they add just the right amount of modern glamour. And if you want to amp up the fancy factor in any room, our go-to is a pretty pendant like the one we used in the walk-in robe.

ADD ARCHITECTURAL DETAIL

Attaching simple panelling to plasterboard can elevate a room and give it a boutique hotel feeling faster than you can say, 'Room for two, please.' It's an easy way to turn a plain wall into something more interesting. And – even better – it's kind on the budget. If you're handy on the tools, this is even something you could DIY.

Bring on
the bling!
Gold taps and sconces
act like jewellery in
this bathroom.

BLACK + BLACK

A black sink + black vanity is a strong combo. In this feminine room, it anchors the space – making it feel balanced and modern.

A LOO WITH A VIEW

We know, we know! Putting a feature window next to a toilet is a big call, but hear us out: that window creates architectural interest *and* floods the room with natural light, making it feel so much bigger. And installing a motorised awning on the other side of this window means that privacy is at your fingertips. At the push of a button – 'Hey presto!' – you can see out, but no one can see in. The only blushes here are on the tiles.

Hot tip

If you're going with a bold floor tile, then let it be the diva it was born to be by using neutral tiles – like these pink and cream diamonds – on the other surfaces.

SLIMLINE STORAGE

Don't overlook the bonus space to be had inside a mirrored cabinet when looking to add storage to bathrooms. The high-maintenance partner (there's always one) can claim the roomier vanity, leaving the cabinet shelves free for their low-maintenance partner.

ENCAUSTIC-LOOK FLOOR TILES

We had our eye on these tiles for a while, so we had to use them in this house. They LOOK like olde-worlde encaustic tiles, but they are actually porcelain. True encaustic tiles have been around for centuries – they're those gorgeous, patterned clay tiles you find in old European buildings. The beauty of modern porcelain tiles is that they are cheaper and more durable than encaustic ones, meaning that you can achieve this amazing look for less. Plus, when you touch them, they have a lightly textured surface, so they feel really nice underfoot. That's a winner for us – especially in bathrooms.

"I smile every time I see this room. This was a spare bedroom, but it backed onto the new alfresco area. Once we added some double French doors, it screamed 'entertaining area'.

"The wallpaper is the true star of the show. With a pattern like this, I knew that I couldn't have another strong pattern in the room – it would have created visual confusion. Instead, I went with pared-back gold, cream and white, and a few black accents. I joined two gold shelving units to create a wall of bling, and then I only needed a few touches to finish things off.

"I mixed a few styles in this room: tropical wallpaper, French country-style armchairs, Aztec patterned cushions and an Art Deco wall unit. It sounds like a lot, but it works!"

Bonnie

The beauty of this room is that it can easily be changed into a study or bedroom down the track. This type of flexibility is becoming more and more important in family homes, as kids leave home or (let's be real) move back in!

Cluster pretty pieces at either end of a sideboard to give the wall hero its moment in the spotlight.

DOUBLE UP

If your budget doesn't stretch to the extra-long sideboard of your dreams, then you may be able to cheat by pushing two smaller sideboards together, like we did. It has the same big impact, offers loads of storage and is kinder on the budget.

PICTURES DON'T NEED TO BE MATCHY MATCHY

As long as you use similar frames and make sure the colours in the images work beautifully together and with the tones in the room, you can absolutely hang two different pieces side by side. In fact, we encourage it. It's a great way to add interest.

<<<

MAKE THE MOST OF THIS STYLING 'MOMENT'

A sideboard can be a real moment, so be strategic when styling it. We recommend starting with a wall hero – this can be a painting, wall hanging or a print you love – then building around that. Next, choose a few decorative pieces of varying heights.

High pieces: Adding height to a sideboard is the most important thing to do because that's going to help balance out the long, slimline dimensions of most sideboards. Our go-to is a vase of flowers or stems, but a plant or a table lamp is also perfect for bringing in height. We like to position taller pieces so that they overlap the wall art slightly and create a visual connection.

Mid-height pieces: These are often sculptural pieces. We love using empty vases, succulents or large candles.

Low-lying pieces: For these, we often use pretty bowls, mud beads, candles, a small stack of books or some things from nature – shells, coral or a small piece of driftwood.

A console and a mirror transform a bare wall into a beautiful moment.

GO LOW

Placing a couple of things on the lower shelves rather than leaving them empty will help make things look 'finished'. If you have a lot of empty space under a console or shelving unit, you might want to slide a footstool or basket underneath to round out the look.

White works!

White grout helps this herringbone pattern pop. And white towels will always be #classic.

Shout-out to the design moguls at Missoni for this pattern inspo.

HERRINGBONE DREAMS

From graphic herringbone tile patterns to bold black accents, we pushed the envelope in every direction in this bathroom. The result is luxury that makes a real statement.

TOP-HEAVY TREATMENT

A shaving cabinet with generous storage is an easy way to balance out a bare-as-bones vanity. Everyone gets their own shelf – problem solved!

THIS PERGOLA IS PURELY FOR THE PRETTY

We know what you're thinking: 'Why does this pergola have no cover?' It definitely *could* have one, but we built it for the architectural look and feel rather than as a practical weather cover. When you're designing, give yourself permission to think outside the square and make some decisions purely for how they'll look. It's okay if a few things skew more towards 'form' than 'function' – they'll contribute massively to how the finished house looks and feels.

100

*Pergola + privacy screen =
outdoor oasis*

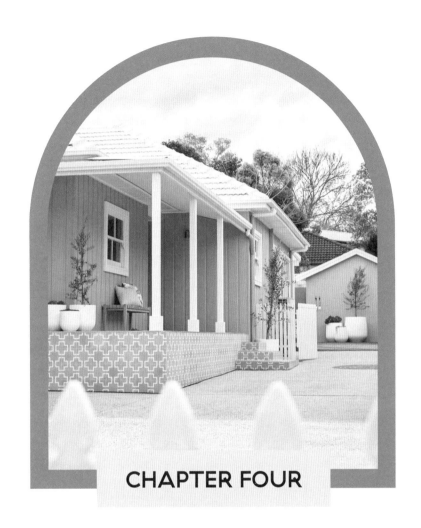

CHAPTER FOUR

Contemporary
COTTAGE

OUR FAIRYTALE RENO!

When we put out a call asking if anyone in Sydney wanted us to renovate their home, we never imagined that our inbox would be overflowing with messages from over 800 people submitting their homes for consideration. We were blown away! Especially because there was a bit of a catch: they'd need to hand over their keys, their budget and full creative control to us.

After days of deliberating and comparing all of the submissions, we found our diamond in the historic town of Windsor. This dated little cottage on a busy main road with a flight path overhead was a true renovator's delight. She was the right size, shape and location, and was in dire need of some TLC. Even better, the reno timeline meant that we'd be able to wedge this project into our already jam-packed schedule (hence our affectionate nickname for her: our 'Windsor Wedgie').

Modern mums Sarah and Cath, along with their two sons Chaise and Addison, gave us their keys, their budget and their blessing, and off we went. From the front fence to the backyard, we transformed their cute cottage into a warm, stylish and low-maintenance family home they'll love for years to come.

We welcomed them back to their home by throwing them an intimate and unforgettable backyard wedding ... and they all lived happily ever after.

BEFORE

AFTER

DON'T FRET THE FRETWORK

Decorative fretwork can be beautiful. Sometimes you need to keep it, and the end result can be amazing. At other times, it pays to be ruthless and fully committed to your vision board. On this house, the fretwork was dating the cottage and keeping it rooted in the past while we were trying to lead it towards a cleaner, more contemporary future. The fretwork had to go for the greater good. These decisions shouldn't be hard. Your vision board will hold the answers.

CLAD UP FOR CONTEMPORARY

One of the MOST important design decisions when it came to modernising this cottage was changing the direction of the cladding. Running the cladding vertically rather than horizontally helps to update period cottages in a way that looks fresh and new without sacrificing character.

BEFORE

CHUNK UP WINDOW TRIMS

If you aren't changing the windows, consider updating their trims. It's easy, it freshens up the facade, and it gives your windows real presence. We gave these babies a thick fibre-cement trim that's easy to attach around existing window frames. It makes the windows POP and has the added benefit of being a hard-wearing and low-maintenance material.

GO FOR GOLD

It's the cherry on top of the pretty icing on that delicioso cake. Gold trim is definitely not a must-have, but there's no doubt that it takes the look up a few notches. Best of all, it's not expensive! We bought it from the local hardware store.

SAY HELLO TO SEXY NEW TILES

There's no better way to pretty up an entry than with some drop-dead gorgeous tiles. They can really take a boring concrete porch to next-level amazing. The decision to tile the vertical front face of the porch was made at the last minute, but we've got to say that we think it totally makes the entire porch!

THE POWER OF THREE

One of our fave outdoor styling tricks is grouping three pots together with a variety of green, non-flowering plants. It never lets us down. For this house, rather than choosing plants with glossy, bright green leaves (such as banana palms, which we adore), we went for plants with a muted, grey–green colour to better tie in with the hue of the house.

From cream to green

Dulux 'Pozieres' is a soft-as-a-whisper colour that pays homage to the heritage of Windsor while also giving this little cottage a fresh start.

Adding super-simple timber bump outs (aka 'shrouds') around the base of these front posts makes them look finished and more substantial.

Gold trim

TIMELESS TIMBER

When you hear 'timber kitchen', most people visualise a country-style or rustic kitchen. But timber transcends time and can look equally at home in a contemporary kitchen with slimline profiles and modern touches.

ISLAND WAVES

If you want an island bench that makes a statement, why not really give people something to talk about? This unique triple-curved-front island with timber slats and floating finish is a bit of a show stopper. Not many islands look like they're suspended in the air. And because we had plenty of seating options within arm's length of this island – a servery right outside the kitchen window, a bench seat opposite the island and a dining table a few steps from the kitchen – we were able to forgo island seating, which also helps to keep the focus squarely on this stand-alone piece.

BENCHTOP TRENDS

One minute, thick benchtops are all the rage. Next minute, thin is in. We never follow these trends. Our advice is to choose the thickness that works best with your vision and your budget. We went with 20 mm leather-honed stone on these benchtops, but we've also been known to use 20 mm, 60 mm AND 300 mm thick benchtops within 12 months of each other. In general, thinner benchtops are more affordable than thicker ones, unless you're going super slim – like 12 mm. Those can actually be pricier than the 20 mm cuts.

Hot tip

If you've got a statement feature in a room, accentuate it with styling accessories that tie in with it. Can you spot all of the round/curved items? They're hard at work highlighting our wavy island.

To create cohesion in a space, choose a detail to repeat in a few spots. The timber grooved-strip detailing in this sculptural island is echoed up in the integrated rangehood, in the grooved face of the farmhouse sink and in the cladding on the upper walls. This room works because the pieces within it are all speaking the same stylish language.

Laundry hidden here!

LEAVE ROOM IN YOUR LAYOUT

Be sure to allow ample space in the walkways around your island, *especially* if you're going to be opening a dishwasher into that aisle. We reckon that a 1.2-metre wide walkway is ideal, and we wouldn't go any tighter than 1 metre.

DITCH THE LAUNDRY ROOM

Renovating is about compromise. We say this all the time, because it's true! No matter how big or small your house, or how tiny or huge your budget. And that's where your list of priorities comes into play. Once you know what matters most to you, hard decisions become easier to make. Would we have loved to create a spacious laundry room with access to the garden in this house? Of course! But doing that would have stolen significant space from the kitchen or another room in the house, which we deemed MORE important. So we said *sayonara* to the spacious laundry, and *hola* to the Euro! A laundry this conveniently located will make it easy to stay on top of the washing and give every member of the family more room to move every single day. #noregrets

The perfect
coffee spot
#YESWAYLATTE

CONNECTION CUES

When spaces are connected, it's important that they link to each other visually, too. The modern white pendant and white trim on the rattan chairs here link to the hits of white in the gorgeous sofa and accent pieces in the lounge beyond.

THE MAGIC OF ASYMMETRY

With that arch and that centred pendant light, symmetrical styling would have been the most obvious direction to take. But we wanted to keep this space feeling relaxed, so we went the asymmetrical route – hanging art on one side of the arch and popping a tall olive tree on the other. Now, everything works together to make one beautifully balanced room.

FLOOR TO CEILING

Getting your curtains the perfect length is pretty damn important. Nothing is worse than curtains that are too short (okay, wait: artwork that's hung too high is definitely worse). Your curtains should skim the ground. If in doubt, go a tad longer. It's A-OK if they bend a bit at the bottom. If we're being really honest (we're all friends here), these curtains could have been *juuuust* a touch longer – like 20 mm longer. See how we also installed the curtain rail as high as possible (just under the cornice)? This gives the illusion of bigger windows and higher ceilings. The curtains and blinds MAKE this moment. Could you imagine the space without them?

If a load-bearing wall is cramping your open-plan
style, removing it shouldn't feel scary. Discuss
it with your builder: find out what's involved and
how much it's going to cost to make it happen.
Your dream style is worth fighting for.

MOVE OVER WHITE PAINT (TEMPORARILY, ANYWAY)

We've fallen in love with this warmer tone. We went top to toe with it – including trims and ceiling – and now walking into this room is like slipping into a warm hug (who doesn't need that right about now?). It just makes us feel so GOOD!

ARCH-ITECTURAL ZONING

This little cottage already had some baby curves of its own, so we embraced them and added a few more, including the big mumma curve dividing the living and dining rooms. These curves were made using flexible plasterboard – what a great material. A statement arch is a superb way to divide rooms while also adding some serious wow factor.

TWO-WAY BENCH SEATS

We'd never put a bench seat – let alone a *two-way* bench seat – smack bang in the middle of an arch before, but we're now sold on the idea! It's a beautiful way to separate two spaces while maintaining a connection between them (pretty smart, hey?) and providing hidden storage (even smarter!). We're willing to bet that it's one of the best seats in the house when there's a party.

SMOKE SHOW!

We swapped the cottage's traditional glossy cypress pine floors for a smoky oak engineered timber, which works so well with our new colour palette. This was 100 per cent the right choice. Without making this change, these rooms would feel totally different – and not in a good way.

"The ideal height for bench seats has been a hot topic at Three Birds HQ for several years now, and after much deliberation and measuring, we feel good saying that 500 mm is the optimum bench-seat height. But the watchout here is if you're including a cushion. In that case, the bench seat should be built a touch lower to ensure that the finished height (including the cushion topper) is no more than 500 mm. And when it comes to depth, the ideal is 400 mm. We literally had the builder measure my bum to make sure. #truestory – check out page 255 for proof."

BEFORE

FROM HARDLY WORKING TO HARDWORKING FEATURE

An old fireplace can add instant character to a room, but if it's seen better days, don't be afraid to close it in and update it (unless you're in a cold climate, of course). This home had ducted heating already, so we pulled out the electric heater that had been shoved in the fireplace and painted the whole thing – chimney and surrounds – in the same colour as the walls using a special acrylic texture paint that is applied like render to the brickwork. Now this fireplace is basically a fixed piece of furniture. It's the perfect spot to display some gorgeous ceramics and is ready for some Chrissy mantelpiece love come December (see pages 206–7 for inspo).

ROUND OFF

Using accessories and furniture with curves offsets the sharp angles in a room. The accessories we've put above and inside this fireplace are all rounded for exactly this reason.

'ART' DOESN'T HAVE TO MEAN ARTWORK

A beautiful painting or print might be perfect for your room, but a sculptural mirror, woven hanging, soft juju hat or special item you have fallen in love with can also satisfy this brief. Case in point, the gorgeous gold-rimmed mirror above the mantelpiece.

The blinds on either side of
the fireplace are to this lounge
room what filters are to photos.
These ones bring instant glow.
#wokeuplikethis

Dulux 'Deep Sun' has us swooning.

HOLD YOUR NERVE

If you choose a bold colour for a room (and FYI, a kid's room is the perfect place to do this), then you might find yourself second-guessing your choice. Probably after the paint is on the walls. But DO NOT judge the room until *everything* has gone in and you've styled it up. You need the furniture, linens, art and accent pieces to help you tell the story and bring that strong colour down to earth. It's the timber, rattan and textural details that make this mustard feel so warm and livable. Stick to your guns, style that room, and THEN judge away!

DON'T FORGET THE FUN FACTOR

Styling a kid's bedroom is a great opportunity to bring in a lighthearted feature. It doesn't need to be anything crazy, just something that's going to make their friends say, 'Cool!' when they walk through the door. For this pre-teen, a custom-made half-pipe bed (packed to the roof with storage – literally!) more than met that brief. It provides a focal point for the room and delivers on the cool factor.

THINGS ARE LOOKING UP!

Patterned wallpaper on the ceiling? Absolutely! It draws the eye up and is the perfect partner for the mustard walls.

Sleep like a king

The bed fits a king single mattress,
which is the same length as an adult
king-size bed at 203 cm – so there's
plenty of room for this growing boy
to stretch his legs.

Timber wall battens are an easy way to bring architectural detailing and texture to a plain wall. They were the only add-on this room needed to make it feel special.

SHOW OFF THOSE CURVES

Bathrooms are one of the 'hardest' rooms in a home, because they're full of hard and often angular materials such as tiles, stone, marble, metal and glass. We always try to soften these spaces in some way; in this case, curves were the answer. Arching the window, using flexible plasterboard to create a curved wall on one side of the ceiling, adding a rounded nib wall and bringing in that bathtub and beautiful tapware gave us the curvefest we were chasing. A softer and gentler effect was achieved.

CREATE YOUR OWN PRIVATE HANGING GARDEN

A vertical garden is one of the most effective antidotes to a dreary outlook. You don't need to run it the length of the fence, either. Just hang it directly outside the window so it fills your view with lush green goodness, and then enjoy the calming effects. As if that wasn't easy enough, you can even buy self-watering vertical gardens that do the hard work for you, allowing your plants to grow quickly and healthily.

DOUBLE THE GROUT, DOUBLE THE FUN

To create visual interest, we doubled the size of the horizontal grout lines between the tiles. The thick lines are a chunky 15 mm wide. If your tiler baulks at that (ours did), just show him or her this pic. It's proof that it can be done. We're loving the way these thick lines really show off the gorgeous grout colour, which perfectly matches the microcement on the walls and ceiling (turn the page for the full story on microcement).

WELCOME TO THE DAY SPA

Our vision for this main bathroom included a neutral colour palette full of natural tones and textures, and soft day-spa vibes. Throw a fluffy robe and some essential oils into the mix, and you've got yourself one heavenly little escape.

COST IT ALL

When costing up your bathroom reno, budget for everything: toilet-roll holder, towel rail, robe hooks, door stopper ... Every. Last. Detail.

Make grout a feature!

"Open shower concepts really look the goods, but they've GOT to function well, too. The key to nailing functionality is working out the correct 'fall' on the floor so that all of the water runs back into the shower and towards the drain. Here, a strip drain works much better than a small square one, because it catches a lot more water. It's easier to direct water into a long strip than a small hole."

Erin

MICROCEMENT IS MAJOR!

To bring our vision of a soft bathroom to life, we did some things that we've never done in a bathroom before. The one with the biggest impact was using microcement for the walls and ceiling. Microcement is a combo of cement and resins. It's applied in several very thin layers in much the same way as render to create a seamless look. It's strong AND water resistant, and visually it creates the most perfect texture – one that's so soft to the touch ... dare we say, 'suede-y'. Just look at the way the light dances across it.

Microcement is a good choice for areas that are directly exposed to water, such as showers and vanities. It's flexible so it won't crack due to movement, and perfect for curved features such as our nib wall. But perhaps its GREATEST quality is that it doesn't require any joins, which makes cleaning and maintenance very easy. See you later, soap scum! This misty grey colour was custom blended for us – it matches the colour of the grout – and we're willing to bet that there's a perfect shade for your bathroom, too.

BRONZE IS THE WINNER HERE

When we're talking tapware, bronze certainly doesn't mean third place! This colour is an absolute winner, especially next to the soft curves of the shower. This tapware was custom coated with a 'Living Rustic Bronze' finish to give it the warm, earthy look we were seeking. The bronze is living, which means that it will age and develop a beautiful patina over time.

GET THAT SHOWERHEAD HEIGHT RIGHT FIRST TIME

Fixed showerheads look great, and their unfussy appearance makes them especially well suited to bathrooms with a more minimalist look. But since they can't be adjusted the way rail showers can be, they've got to be installed at the right height first time around. We think that the right height is anything between 2000 and 2200 mm high. Sometimes, we like to ask a tall tradie to stand in the space for us while we mark it out with our plumber.

WHY THE WALL?

This nib wall offers a few big benefits. Not only does it hide the toilet from view (ALWAYS a must for us), but it's also high enough and wide enough (1680 mm high by 1100 mm wide) to account for shower overspray, and this allowed us to skip the shower screen completely. This approach for an open-concept wet area totally brought our day-spa vision to life.

Blush grout!

THROW SOME SHAPES

Did you know that your shower screen doesn't have to be rectangular? Glass can easily be custom cut to your desired shape (within reason, of course). The arch on the glass echoes the curves used throughout the main bedroom and makes it feel like a soft, feminine space.

GET WET WHEN YOU MEAN TO, AND NOT A SECOND BEFORE

Mixers are often installed directly under showerheads out of habit, but this is something you want to put some thought into. Notice how we've positioned these ones to the right of the shower (no wet arms here!) yet still in reach of the shower so the temperature can easily be adjusted once you're in. You'll want to map out your mixer position before the rough-in stage. That way, you won't be stuck having to make a snap decision about placement while your plumber waits to cut the hole.

ARE YOU TEAM OPEN OR CLOSED?

Open ensuites (i.e. ensuites with no door on them) are always conversation starters. Most of the ensuites we've designed are within a stone's throw of the bedroom and don't have doors on them (gasp!). This feels completely normal to us. If you're on the fence, why not hang a gorgeous floor-to-ceiling curtain across the opening and have the best of both worlds?

CREATE SEAMLESS TRANSITIONS

The wall with the arched niche is a great example of how to create a seamless transition from bedroom to bathroom. It's not a tiled wall, so it feels more like a continuation of the bedroom, even though it's technically sitting within the footprint of the bathroom. A wall like this makes the transition from bedroom to bathroom look and feel much more gradual. Imagine if it had been tiled.

WHAT A COMPLEMENT!

This gorgeous piece of art complements the colours and tones of this bedroom perfectly. It picks up on hues used in the room and makes a statement without making a statement, you know?

> ★ DIY HACK ★
>
> *Champagne wardrobes*
>
> Adding decorative moulding to standard wardrobe doors has to be one of the easiest ways to update and elevate them. It worked a treat on these wardrobes. We added fabulous arch-detail moulding, painted the doors a pretty colour, finished with some gorgeous handles and *voilà!* Total transformation.

The pleather bedhead is the focal point of the room and its lines draw your eyes up to the high ceilings.

BEFORE

LET THE GOOD TIMES ROLL

The back of this house was stuck in a dark place. The deck was wobbly and rotten, the grass was struggling to find light, and the yard was constantly muddy. Now it's light, bright and low maintenance. The zones we created all connect to each other in a way that feels inviting and quirky. It's a magnet for good times.

PERGOLAS SCRUB UP WELL

If your previously perky pergola is down in the dumps, give it a weekend of your time and some elbow grease, and prepare to be wowed. After we removed two pillars from the middle of the deck to open things up, all this one needed was a fresh coat of paint and a few sheets of new polycarbonate roofing, and we were back in business, baby.

FOREVER FLAWLESS

Fake turf has come a *very* long way since the scratchy, plasticky stuff you'd find on playgrounds back in 'the day'. Today's artificial grass re-creates the feeling of soft, natural grass and looks perfect from day one. This backyard gets a lot of shade, and we didn't want to risk mud and grass being traipsed through the house. Enter this gorgeous green lawn, which feels great on the tootsies and requires little to no maintenance. Years from now, it will still look this good.

SAND AHOY!

How pretty is this sandy-coloured deck? We love how the black strips in HardieDeck make it look like a boat deck. #instantcoastalvibes

TIMBER + FRESH AIR WERE MADE FOR EACH OTHER

When it comes to outdoor furniture, timber is (literally!) made for the great outdoors. It links back to nature, brings warmth and texture to the space, and silvers beautifully when left in the elements.

We softened the hard angles of the rectangular table and deck by styling with circular homewares.

Notice all the curves we used outside? They help to create a connection with the inside of the home.

RE-USE YOUR BRICK PAVERS

If you're pulling up brick pavers in your backyard, don't toss them. They make fantastic garden borders, like the wavy one we created around these crushed white pebbles.

BLOCK PARTY

Breeze (aka besser) blocks are patterned concrete blocks best known from 1950s Palm Springs architecture. They're an inexpensive way to bring a happy holiday feeling to the most suburban of spaces.

USE CUSHIONS TO CREATE CONNECTION

Pretty outdoor cushions have to be one of the easiest ways to create that all-important connection between the indoor and outdoor spaces. Simply look at the colours and patterns you've used inside the house, then buy outdoor cushions in those same tones and patterns (in a weather-resistant fabric with mould-resistant filling, of course).

Say hello to the spritz shed!

TAKE YOUR SHED FROM HUMBLE TO HELL YEAH!

Who needs a place to store a whipper snipper when you can enjoy a gin and tonic party with friends? Actually, there's still storage in the back of this shed for those non-party essentials. If you're a social animal who likes to entertain at home, a 'spritz shed' might be just what's missing from your life. But if parties aren't your jam, then a cute yoga studio or a creative space with an easel and paints could be equally as gorgeous. Garden sheds are little rooms with big potential. The only limit is your imagination.

Our curved splashback ties back to the curves in the house.

CLUSTER THOSE POTS

Grouping potted plants on a deck or near an entrance – anywhere, really! – adds bursts of greenery without the hassle and cost of planting garden beds. Bright white pots look incredible against both dark and light colours. You can't go wrong!

A SIDE PROFILE TO LOVE

Grained cladding (vertical, to match the house) gives this shed some texture and dials up those outdoor vibes. The pretty touch comes courtesy of those gorgeous hooks and gardening tools.

CHAPTER FIVE

Australian
STAYCATION

ACREAGE LIVING NEVER LOOKED SO GOOD

'Cancel your plane tickets, we're bringing the holiday to you!' That's the message this house is sending, and it's impossible to resist. #passtheSPF! The brief for this new build – our most ambitious one yet – was to create a family home that was functional for daily life but also felt like being on a dream holiday. And if this sprawling home doesn't say 'idyllic island getaway', we don't know what does! With its grand entrance, tall palms, high ceilings, textural touches and sparkling pool, this house has luxury resort moments on tap.

Inside, we took a more eclectic approach than we usually do, mixing styles to give rooms their own personalities, but weaving the same colour palette throughout. Modern and traditional touches live side-by-side, masculine and feminine styling complement each other, and minimalist rooms live happily down the hall from maximalist ones. But, at the end of the day, these rooms are all anchored by one thing: views of that iconic Aussie bush. Like a living piece of art that can be seen from almost every window in the house, it connects the spaces to each other, and to the paradise outside. #timeforatrip #outofoffice

Checkmate!

CONTRAST CREATES IMPACT

The placement of black roof tiles against a pristine white house makes such a strong statement. Accentuate this contrast even more by adding other black details, like we've done with the outdoor lights.

GOING GRAND? SYMMETRY IS YOUR FRIEND

We mirrored everything down to the potted plants to create an entrance with a grand, resort-like feel. The super-high roofline only adds to the sense of drama.

SLIGHTLY OBSESSED WITH BOARD-AND-BATTEN WALLS

If you want a coastal holiday vibe for the exterior of your home but you don't want to use super-popular weatherboard cladding, then you should consider the board-and-batten look we've used here. As the name suggests, it simply comprises large, flat sheets of cladding (the boards) with vertical trims (the battens) on top. The battens create stylish detailing, and they also help to cover the joins in the boards.

GIVE US GREEN!

When we close our eyes and think 'holiday', we see green palms swaying in the breeze, emerald jungles and lush trailing plants. For that reason, large potted palms were a must-have item in our budget. We went for tropical plants such as Bangalow, cycad and raffia palms. Because we preferred to have established plants, we had to save a lot of our budget for big plants and big pots. But it was so worth it. This house would feel completely different without them.

REIMAGINE A CLASSIC

Chequerboard floors have been making bold statements in entryways for thousands of years (seriously, we checked!). By swapping out the traditional black and white tiles for a blush pink and white combo, we softened the strong pattern and made it subtler.

141

Love your outdoor tiles? Continue them inside like we did here for a seamless connection between inside and out.

<<<

ROOM TO MOVE

A gorgeous table is a great way to anchor a large entryway. Just make sure you can walk comfortably around it. And keep the styling simple and pretty. If it's likely to become a collecting spot for keys, wallets and sunnies, find a large vessel such as a clamshell to contain all of those bits and bobs in a beautiful way.

Styling pieces echo the scallop shape of the pendant above.

French glass doors give this entire space detail and are a practical way to create some privacy in the study.

OPTICAL ILLUSION

The pendant in the office looks centred when you view it from the entryway, but it's not. We actually hung it off-centre over the desk. When you are in the office, this off-centre placement creates a feeling of more space at the other end of the desk

DROP IT LIKE IT'S HOT

Unlike when we hang pendants over a kitchen island or dining table, we don't follow a hard and fast rule when it comes to hanging a pendant in an entryway. How low you go should be guided by what's going on beneath that pendant. Since nobody will be walking under this one, we were able to hang it quite low and create a more intimate feeling.

GO BIG OR GO HOME

You can't go wrong with an oversized pot in a large entryway, but it has to be BIG so it can hold its own in that vast space. Whether you fill it with pampas grass or branches, or leave it empty, it acts like a sculpture.

SWAP CHAIRS FOR STOOLS

Give visitors to your office a cool stool to perch on rather than a chair. This will make the room look bigger, and the stools can be tucked neatly under the desk when not in use. (And, let's be honest, if your guests aren't able to lie back and lose focus in a soft, comfy lounge, your meetings might be shorter and more efficient. That's another tick for firm stools.)

This room wouldn't have felt so grand if we'd hung the curtains directly above the window.

The symmetrical arrangement of the furniture creates a formal feeling, but the large rattan rug, soft neutral tones, oversized linen loungers and organic-shaped coffee tables make this a space in which you can relax.

Greenery brings this room to life and connects it with the divine Aussie bush outside.

MIRROR IMAGE

The back of the house is just as impressive and beautiful as the front. We even used the same exterior lights in the same place on the pillars to create a mirror-image effect. Now, the owners can soak up an incredible view of their home from the comfort of their backyard.

TURF FOR A TROPICAL LOOK

If a holiday vibe is all over your vision board, then a simple and cost-effective way to landscape your garden – especially when tackling a big section – is to turf as much as possible. Grass looks great, has a massive impact and doesn't cost as much as garden beds and planting.

Ah, the serenity ...
#NATURE

HOW TO CREATE A SOCIABLE POOL

Different levels and ledges in a pool will make it a sociable space for swimmers and loungers. This pool has steps at one end and a long ledge that runs along the side. Parents can sit at the top and enjoy a cheeky martini, or lounge along the ledge while the kids splash about. If you're planning a pool with entertaining in mind, ledges (or swim-outs, as they're called in the pool biz) are a great option.

CAN YOU SPOT THE SPIGOTS?

You can't, right? That's because this glass pool fence is not only 'frameless' but also 'channel set'. This means that it's been installed into a trough cut into the tiles, so it doesn't require metal spigots to hold the panels of glass in place. This method of installation is more expensive than regular fencing, but if uninterrupted views and a truly frameless glass fence are on your wish list, then it's the way to go.

IT'S NOT ROCKET SCIENCE

Around the pool, we went with black umbrellas and white trim to match the contrast between the roof and the exterior colour of the pool house. Colour matching doesn't have to be hard.

SLIDING STACKERS

What's better than bi-fold doors? Sliding stackers that vanish completely inside a pocket cavity.

151

A good electrician will be able to retrofit fans in your existing outdoor roof if you love the holiday feeling they create. Breeze ahoy!

★ DIY HACK ★

Textured paint to the rescue

Rendering bricks can cost time and money, so try a textured paint instead. We used this type of paint to cover these brick columns, as well as the breeze-block walls of the contemporary cottage (see page 133). It gives a perfectly imperfect finish that we just love. #winwin

CREATING AN OUTDOOR CONNECTION

If you have a wide house rather than a tall house (perhaps it's single level), then look for an opportunity to include a back porch or deck that runs the full width of the house. Consider adding doors to each room so that they open up onto the porch to maximise indoor/outdoor living.

Open up your world

Bi-fold windows off a
kitchen instantly add beauty
and practicality to any home.
They turned this corner into
an extremely sociable
and open zone.

GAS IT UP!

A gas-strut window is a no-brainer when planning a barbecue area next to an indoor space. It creates connection and conversation like nothing else. Some people might think it's strange to put one right next to another huge opening, like the sliding door here, but connecting spaces isn't just about physically joining them, it's also about how people behave in those areas. Now, thanks to this gas-strut window, anyone sitting on the tall seats outside will be connected to people lounging inside on the day bed. That link will keep the drinks, food and conversation flowing, which is what alfresco living is all about!

LOUNGE-LOVER'S DELIGHT

This curvy day bed makes such good use of this nook. Now it's the perfect spot to escape the sun and curl up with a book. Our builder framed this up for us, and then we used timber mouldings on the face of the base (and the bar next door) to add interest, texture and that wavy effect. If you're wondering how we found a foam pad to exactly match this curvy shape, we just got lucky! Nah, just joking! We had it made.

SHE SAYS SEASHELLS ...

The low-hanging seashell pendant creates a warm and intimate mood when the sun goes down. The shells add to the beachy poolside ambience, especially when they tinkle softly as they sway in the wind. #feeltheserenity

A view so nice we framed it twice!

This streamlined barbecue is barely noticeable, and we love that.

CHOOSE ART THAT REFLECTS THE SETTING

The print above the bar is such a focal point in this pool house. One peek in this direction, and it immediately draws the eye. We took the opportunity to play up the connection to the pool by choosing an underwater shot. Art can create an instant sense of place, so always consider the feeling you want to evoke in a room and then look for art that supports your vision.

OCEAN PEARL

If you hear the phrase 'pearlescent shimmer' and think of frosted lipstick and nail salons, then it's time we introduced you to the powers of pearlescent paint. After adding scalloped timber moulding to the front of the bar, we painted the whole thing a pearlescent white, which looks incredible when the sun hits it. This isn't the type of paint you'd go slapping on every wall; however, when used sparingly, it provides a subtle pearly shimmer that catches the eye, especially on curved surfaces.

SEA-FOAM DREAMS

Laying these refreshing square tiles in a diamond pattern gives this bathroom personality – you've got to have a bit of fun in a pool-house bathroom. When you're using colour as a feature in one area, it's always a good idea to keep the other colours in that room quite neutral.

LOOKS LIKE A BAR, ACTS LIKE A KITCHEN

You'd never know that this pool house doubles as guest accommodation, and that's because we've styled it to look like a bar rather than the fully functioning kitchen and laundry it is. By building the bar taller than a traditional kitchen island, the kitchen-y appliances are hidden from view. Using louvred doors rather than regular kitchen cabinetry also helps the room look more cabana than catering. There's a pantry, kettle and toaster concealed behind one set of doors, and a laundry tucked behind the other.

WATERPROOF YOUR SHOWER WINDOW

You absolutely CAN have a window in your shower, but any old window won't do. The glass must meet a certain standard, and the opening must be lined and waterproofed prior to installation. These powder-coated aluminium windows won't rust, so they're a great choice for this room. And to up the protection even more, the window trim and architraves have been primed and then painted in a semi-gloss enamel paint. If showering by sunlight feels a little out there, external privacy awnings outside will lower at the push of a button.

Cladding and shell sconces give this bathroom a beachside feel.

It was a toss-up between a pendant and a palm in this corner. In the end, we chose a pygmy palm to bring a holiday feeling to this room.

A big, beautiful bench seat behind the table makes this room more useful and versatile. It's an inviting nook at any time of the day or night.

What perfect looks like when it comes to rug size.

ELEVATE FAMILY SPACES

Choosing soft, sculptural pieces for the lounge room is an easy way to make it look drop-dead gorgeous. The feature chair and raw, sculptural coffee table not only warm up this room, but also help to tie it in with what's happening in the rest of the house.

STAY A WHILE

Creating a dining area in which people will be happy kicking back is all about introducing soft shapes and inviting textures. A super-plush rug and two sculptural bouclé chairs make this a room that nobody will be in a rush to leave. If you use lounge chairs at a dining table, then you need to ensure that they're high enough for the diners to comfortably reach the table.

The shapes in the pendant soften the hard kitchen and echo the pendant in the entrance. Creating these visual connections is important.

THINK OUTSIDE THE SQUARE

We could have put a huge piece of art on this wall, but it would have competed with the oversized pendant, statement chairs and chunky island. Instead, we chose a smaller piece and lined it up with the island bench, rather than centring it on the wall. This placement, along with its earthy tones and coconut theme, create a clear connection to the kitchen space.

CHAIRS CAN TELL A STORY

Using chairs rather than stools in a kitchen gives you a chance to make a real style statement and emphasise that this is a dining space. The shape, texture and colour of these chairs bring so much warmth to this space.

ISLAND DINING

If you don't have enough room for a table in the same area as your kitchen, dropping the level around the island to create a built-in dining table can be a great way to bring the dining and prep area together. There is an art to getting this right, though. The magic is in the millimetres. The height of the island benchtop needs to be right, but the ledge also needs to look good and be tall enough so that anyone sitting at it has clearance for their knees. At 940 mm, this island bench is slightly taller than the standard 900 mm. The table section is 780 mm high.

SWITCH UP THE FLOORING

Don't be afraid to go for a herringbone or chevron pattern for the floorboards if there's a room that needs a boost. We went with a straight lay throughout the rest of the home, but we switched it up in the kitchen space because it just felt right. To transition from a room or hallway that has straight boards into a decorative pattern such as herringbone, we use a thin brass bead to mark the change.

HEIGHT = LUXURY

There were certain areas in this home that needed to feel really luxurious, and this kitchen was one of them. By raking the ceilings, we were able to achieve that feeling of drama in the kitchen, entryway and main ensuite.

Glass and gold

Fluted glass cabinetry with gold handles brings detail and a luxe touch to this functional room, and it looks superb from the kitchen.

If you can get some natural light into your butler's pantry, it will make a huge difference to how you feel in the space. If you can see a palm tree through the window, even better. #palmtherapy #lighttherapy

NEW HOME, OLD-WORLD FEEL

We decided to go for earthy tones throughout this laundry –
including in the gorgeous floor tiles, which have a handmade,
old-world quality to them. Styling the shelf with urn-like
vessels picks up on that old-world look, too.

*Save your back by
elevating your
washer and dryer.*

#NOMOREBENDING

MAXIMISE STORAGE WITHOUT MINIMISING LOOKS

When it comes to storing coats, bags, hats and the outdoor essentials, we are all about maximising storage, but we also like to balance the practical with the pretty. We could easily have built a whole wall of cupboards here, but the bench seat and nook make this space inviting. Now there's a spot to sit while taking shoes off, and there's still storage underneath.

Cupboards with wire fronts hide the mess of family life.

Hot tip

Ventilated cupboards are a must. You have to keep the fresh air flowing around those shoes, boots and coats. We went with sprayed wire instead of rattan for the front of these cupboards. It's a little more durable than rattan, but still has the resort look we were after.

Using different handles throughout the home will add interest, but try to stick to two styles so it doesn't feel too chaotic. We've gone for black handles in some rooms and gold in others.

RÉPÉTEZ S'IL VOUS PLAIT

Repetition is a design power tool that we like to use over and over again. Repeating shapes and colours helps to create cohesion and harmony. In this bathroom, you can see how a simple curve is repeated in the gooseneck showerheads, the shower screens, the basin and the mirror. Together, they offset all of the square angles in the tiles, window and vanity, creating an overall sense of balance.

LEFT OF CENTRE

Placing the basin at one end of the vanity (in this case, it's actually 'right of centre') means that there is more functional bench space available than if we'd plonked it smack bang in the middle, which would be the obvious choice.

MONOCHROMATIC IS NOT MONOTONOUS

A powder room is the one space that your guests are definitely going to visit, so why not make it a real moment? Tone-on-tone colour packs a punch when we allow shape and form to shine, as with this fluted vanity, scalloped stone-look mirror and earth-toned floor tiles. And then we've gone BANG with some gold tapware and that glittery pendant.

WE LOVE A BLING SOUVENIR

Bon bought this gold and glass pendant while on holiday in Bali ... way before this build was even a twinkle in our eye. Her advice? If you're on holiday and see a light fixture you love, buy it! Lighting can always be rewired to your home-country standards. She hauled this one on her back while riding a motorcycle. #commitment

This wall vinyl is anti-mildew and bleach cleanable! It's also exceptionally sustainable, as it's made from recycled raw materials.

FEMININE MEETS MASCULINE

Getting the balance right between masculine and feminine energy in a bedroom can be as simple as going with lighter (feminine) colours for soft furnishings, and darker (masculine) tones for furniture frames. Soft white curtains, bedspread and ottoman pads counteract the rich black of the bed, console table and ottomans. The large art print opposite the bed brings harmony to the room by utilising both light and dark tones, but is void of colour.

ADD RUG MONEY TO YOUR HARDWOOD BUDGET

Floorboards throughout a whole home can be a great move – especially if you have pets. Just remember that you'll need a healthy budget for rugs so you can soften some spaces, especially bedrooms and the lounge room.

YOUR BEDROOM, YOUR RULES

Get playful with the art you choose for your bedroom. We were a little cheeky with this print (literally!), but it works because the tones still fit with the overall theme of the room. Why not have a bit of fun, as it's really for your eyes only?

Oversized art is such an easy way to add interest to a room. This is a tiny wall, but look how big the art is. Without it, this would be a dead space with no personality or purpose. Include a little table with a candle and a few decorative items, and the corner comes to life!

CHOOSE A FEW 'SHOW OFF' SHELVES!

If you want to create some feature shelves in an otherwise closed wardrobe, then those holding your shoes, handbags and sunglasses are the prime ones to show off. These shelves are less likely to look messy and out of control, whereas jeans and T-shirt shelves ... forget it! Adding glass doors and LED strip lighting to your display shelves is an easy way to make them look a million bucks.

"I absolutely LOVE walking into a wardrobe that opens out into a bathroom beyond. That's pure luxury. By placing the bath, wall, mirrors and chandelier in the centre of the walkway, we've made them the focal point whether you're in the bathroom, the wardrobe or the bedroom. From any room, those beautiful elements are framed perfectly."

Bonnie

FANCYPANTS ISLAND?

If budget and space permit, adding an island to your walk-in robe will give you heaps of extra storage, not to mention dial up the luxe factor by 1000 per cent. For an extra-glam finish, we added a stone benchtop (the same stone used in the ensuite that runs off this room).

SUPER SOAKER

Most ensuites don't have enough space for a walk-around bath, so this opportunity was too good to pass up. It's probably the first and only time we'll be able to install a round bath.

LET'S HEAR IT FOR FLOATING VANITY WALLS!

Having a freestanding wall with a shower at one end and a toilet at the other is a functional way of organising a bathroom – and it hides the toilet completely without the need for doors. What more can you ask for? The best thing is that you don't need a huge bathroom to pull this off. For this set-up to work, the floating wall has to be at least 1800 mm wide with a space about 900 mm deep behind it to accommodate the shower and toilet.

WARM UP THE WHITE

If white is the base tone in your bathroom, then layering in beige or creamy colours through tiles, accents and styling will warm up the room. We even brought a soft armchair into the mix. This piece of furniture might feel unexpected in a bathroom, but it's a great way of making the space that little bit softer and cosier.

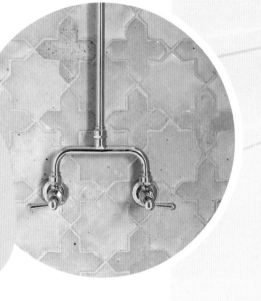

Peachy gold tapware plus these feature tiles is a match made in heaven. Have you noticed how these tiles were repeated in the laundry to create a cohesive feel throughout the home?

This chandelier is not wired up. It's more like a hanging sculpture than a light.

Art with heart: this artwork was painted by the boys' grandmother, making it all the more special.

TIMELESS COLOURS CREATE VERSATILE SPACES

If we asked you how old the occupants of this room are, you'd probably need a minute to look closely at the small details, because these muted colours and eye-catching stripes aren't giving away much! And we bet you wouldn't answer five and eight. From the classic navy ceiling to the neutral, wide stripes and rattan furniture, this room is timeless – and it's easy to see how it will grow with the two young boys who live here. We can definitely see guests feeling right at home here, too! It's a winner across the age groups.

WHAT ROLE DOES YOUR RUG PLAY?

Did you know that the rug is one of the most important design elements in this room, because it visually connects the beds and makes the whole room feel 'together'?

SPOT THE STRIPE

It's no secret that we're obsessed with stripes. You can make them work with any style or setting.

173

If you opt for a feature colour on the ceiling, don't be afraid to take that colour down to the skirting boards as well. It looks great with tall skirting boards, like these ones, but would also work with shorter ones.

For mums of boys, this one's for you! A urinal with sensor flush. #hallelujah

SLEEK SIMPLICITY

Like the ensuite off the main bedroom, the view into this ensuite is also visible from the bedroom and framed by a walkway that takes you through a walk-in robe, but the feeling this time is totally different. At first glance, the white column sink and marble-look tiling seem calm and minimalist, but then you turn right and see the shower, and whoaaa! This brings in an element of surprise and difference, an unexpected moment that is really delightful in a bathroom.

FIND STORAGE SOMEWHERE

If you plan on using a pedestal basin rather than a vanity, ensure that the shaving cabinet has some storage. We also built a ledge along the wall because it's easier for little hands to reach until these boys grow up.

HOW GOOD IS THIS SHOWER?

Walking into a shower and feeling like you're being cocooned is the best. Finger tiles (the long, narrow style we've used here) are your go-to choice when creating curves, because they're easy for your tiler to install around those curves. Penny rounds or other small mosaic tiles would work equally well.

"Please don't forget about the space in your roof when planning your build. #wenearlydid! This beautiful room would have been nothing but roof rafters and storage if we hadn't stuck our heads up here and realised what a big opportunity it was.

"The minute you walk into this bonus living space, you feel relaxed thanks to the wallpaper and huge artwork. And because this is such a large space, we were able to go for two L-shaped lounges (they don't have to match) arranged symmetrically, which links it to the other rooms in the house."

Erin

Skylights are a must in a loft room, because natural light will make the room so much nicer to be in. And if you can splurge on a skylight that opens, do it. The more fresh air and sunshine you can bring into a room, the better. These ones even have retractable blinds for a daytime Netflix binge.

Beige is back!

Dulux 'Vintage Beige' sets a dreamy tone on the walls, while the curved bouclé bedhead, soft linens and plush rug add layers of softness. Even the bedside table is fluffy! This room is like a cloud we want to drift away on.

Simple greenery in a tall vase is an easy way to add height and a pop of colour to any room.

SIDEBOARD CHEAT SHEET

If you get stuck styling a sideboard and the tips on page 99 don't help, then turn to this trio. You really can't go wrong with a piece of art, a stack of books and a vase of greenery for some height. Make sure not to leave a big gap between the frame of the art and the top of the sideboard – remember that artwork should be hung at eye level.

CHAIN STORES CAN DO CUSTOM

Just because you're buying from a chain store doesn't rule out some serious customisation, so it pays to ask what your options are when shopping. This sideboard came from a chain store, but we could change its dimensions, the colour of the timber, the style and colour of the rattan inlay and the handles. #lovethat #affordablecustompieces

CHAPTER SIX

Three Birds
HQ

OUR DIRTY BLUSH CRUSH

Two years after moving into the first Three Birds headquarters, it became clear that our office was due for a makeover. Our team was growing, and we wanted to give our team members (and us!) a luxe, feminine space in which to work. Reno life is chaotic, so our office had to feel calming, cosy and welcoming – a place where we could regroup, think and share ideas.

Our mission for this new HQ was to make it feel more like a home than an office. Key to achieving this vision was the pretty (but gritty) pink colour scheme and some gorgeous pieces of furniture – the kind you'd buy for your home, not the office. Once those things were in place, a few beautiful, decorative touches to inspire creativity pulled everything together.

Every last detail in this office was chosen to make it (and everyone working in it) feel super-special. One week later, we had the collaborative workspace that we'd been dreaming of.

This is where the magic happens.

Mud beads and macramé take the texture in this chandelier to another level.

We designed our HQ around this original painting by Jai Vasicek.

DOUBLE FRAMING, BABY!

If you've got an *ah*-mazing piece of art to hang, consider using timber mouldings to create custom-sized panels on the wall around it, like we've done around this massive painting. Continuing these mouldings throughout the rest of the space not only ensures that the art has pride of place, but it also makes it look perfectly at home on this wall – like it's always been there.

CHOOSE YOUR OWN (WORKSPACE) ADVENTURE

If collaboration is key to your business, encourage that with communal seating and casual work zones. A soft, comfy sofa, gorgeous armchairs and a generous dining table provide plenty of choice. This way, people can choose their spot based on what they're working on, who they're working with and how they're feeling that day. #worklifebalance

Hot tip

Zoning applies to offices, too. Use your office space wisely by zoning it for different purposes – exactly the same way you would in your home or backyard. We created three distinct work zones in our open-plan room. Asymmetrical balance brings a sense of casual living to the space, and each of the zones is styled with clusters of pretty objects: candles, cushions, shiny trinkets and statement lights.

Surprise!

This vase is hiding a secret: there's a power point behind it. Even in the office, Bon is always looking for ways to hide power points!

Our comfy, creative corner.

"Pink on pink isn't the obvious choice for an office space – it's more cocktails and cushions than computers, but that's exactly what we were after! When people think of the colour pink, bright, lolly shades probably come to mind, but our vision was for pink with some grit! A dirty blush base for a gritty but pretty space. The first sample pots we tried on the walls just happened to work perfectly together (gotta love it when that happens!), so we went two-tone with the paint choices to create some dimension in the room. The lighter Dulux 'Ellen Half' was perfect for the floor and the long panels underneath the wallpaper; the deeper, dirtier 'Maiko' was used on the walls and cabinetry."

Lana

Paint the floor?

#YESWAYROSÉ

Best spot in the house for laying out samples and swatches.

WARM UP COMMUNAL SPACES

A large timber table anchors a space, gives it a clear purpose and adds a wealth of warmth to any room. It also flies in the face of traditional office furniture, which usually has a harder, colder feel to it. Hang a pendant or two and bring in decorative pops of gold, and you're well on your way to creating a work zone that feels relaxed, inviting and inspiring.

SIGNS CAN SAY MORE THAN YOU THINK

No matter how small your business is when you're starting out, hanging your company sign on the wall can give you an extra bump of confidence and confirm that you're really 'in business'. As our team has grown and we've welcomed more birdies to the nest, that sign has become even more important – it creates a sense of unity and company.

Hot tip

We've pushed two tables together, because it offers more flexibility and is a lot more affordable than buying a mega table. Now it's our top spot for rolling out floor plans, filming schedules and fabric swatches.

★ DIY HACK ★

A lick of pretty paint

Is your kitchen bland with a capital B? Is the cabinetry in decent shape? If you answered yes to both questions, lucky you! Some DIY energy and a simple lick of cabinetry paint will work a treat. It certainly transformed this kitchenette into a gorgeous little coffee spot.

GO SHOPPING FOR HANDLES

With so many beautiful handles to choose from at every price point, there's no reason to settle for sub-stylish fittings. #spoiledforchoice! It's incredible what a difference swapping out handles can make to the look, feel and functionality of a kitchen. We love these gorgeous half-moons (or tiny tacos).

C'est Bon!

This is Bon's special spot. You'll find her here working from her phone – she hardly ever opens her laptop!

RETHINK OFFICE STORAGE

Steel filing cabinets and industrial bookshelves don't get our creative juices flowing in the same way that a shapely piece of furniture can. This super-pretty cabinet may have been designed with platters and plates in mind, but it's home to our printer paper and stationery now – and it's a delight to look at each day. Which pieces more suited to a home could bring that special touch to your office?

Did somebody say 'after-work aperitif'?

TGIF!

CHAPTER SEVEN

Christmas with
THE BIRDS

HAVE AN EASY, BREEZY CHRISTMAS

Around the same time our northern hemisphere friends begin stocking up on Santa sweaters and woolly socks, we start rolling out the rosé for a summery Chrissy celebration. There are SO many ways to celebrate Christmas Day Down Under – everyone has their own take on it. Whether your family spends it picnicking at the beach, around the table for a traditional lunch or in the backyard enjoying casual canapés, chances are your home will be playing host to a holiday gathering or two – and maybe some house guests. You'll want it looking its festive best.

But understandably, decorating for Christmas can be tough to get right. Especially as many of us grew up in homes where clashing colours on the Christmas tree were all the rage, and there was no such thing as too much tinsel. If tinsel is no longer your jam and you're looking for some serious decorating inspo, you'll love this chapter.

We're partial to a gold, silver and white Christmas theme, which lends itself beautifully to a sunny OR snowy Christmas. We're going to show you how to create an incredible festive feeling in your home while also keeping things stylish, simple and relaxed – just how the holidays should be. We've also got a sackful of hacks to help you save cash for all of those other things on the Christmas list. Let's deck those halls.

Bow-tiful

Give the traditional tree topper the year off, and tie a large linen bow on top of your tree.

Holiday hack
DIY WREATH

There's something so welcoming about seeing a big, beautiful wreath (or several) hanging on a front door or on the walls. With a little DIY energy, you can whip up a wreath that suits your style in a matter of minutes.

YOU'LL NEED:

* A wire wreath and tie wire – you can get both from a garden shop, hardware store or Kmart.
* A faux garland from a home shop + a few pretty stems from garden plants, such as eucalyptus or magnolia.
* Some pine cones or other decorative natural touches (faux berries would also look amazing).

HERE'S HOW YOU DO IT:

* Wrap the garland around the wire wreath, and attach it using tie wire.
* Keep going until you have good coverage, and then cut away any bits you don't need.
* Tie in the individual stems until you get a look you like.
* Tie in a few pine cones or other decorative elements.

Hang up and admire your creation!

Hot tip

For a more authentic wreath, go all natural by using real greenery instead of the faux garland. It won't last longer than the Christmas season, but that doesn't matter. Pull off the greenery when the day is done, and save the wire wreath and ties for next year!

WE'RE DREAMING OF
A WHITE CHRISTMAS

For a natural, beachy Christmas look, keep it simple. We've gone with all-white shells, coral and candles of varying heights and shapes layered over a narrow white table runner. Sand-coloured placemats, gorgeous glasses, stacked plates and gold cutlery finish the look.

We love how you can buy gold cutlery from affordable shops such as Kmart and Target.

Lana calls this her 'Australiana meets Mediterrania' setting.

CREATE A NATURAL(ISH) CENTREPIECE

As you know, one of our fave tricks of the trade is mixing faux plants with real plants. But did you know that we use it for decorating dining tables, too? It can create such an amazing statement centrepiece! Once the rest of the table is styled up, no one will know the difference.

START WITH HEIGHT

A tall platter, unique vase or interesting ice bucket are all great starting points for a table setting. They add height and make a statement, and everything else can work around that.

Santa's elves have style!

Holiday hack

DIY WRAPPING

Not only is this wrapping as cheap as chips (tick), but it's also a great way to introduce neutral tones – or whatever colour theme you're going for – under the tree.

YOU'LL NEED:

- Craft paper
- Linen or raffia
- Some hand-picked greenery or dried flowers from the garden.

HERE'S HOW YOU DO IT:

- Wrap your gifts in craft paper.
- Tear the linen or raffia into 50 mm strips to create a raw edge, and then tie the strips around the wrapped gifts.
- Tuck a sprig of greenery or a dried flower under the bow.

Pile those pretty pressies under the tree!

Heaven sent

If table space is tight,
hang the ice bucket
for the champers
from the pergola.

Holiday hack

HANGING FLORAL ARRANGEMENT

To up the luxe factor, spray-paint the dried palm leaves gold.

Most people forget to look up when they're decorating a dining setting for a special occasion, but what a missed opportunity! Feast your eyes on the floral fantasy hanging over the table here. It brings a celestial feeling and is practically a piece of art – one that looks a million bucks. It's a great holiday hack, and one that's not too tricky to put together. Bon's sons helped her make this one.

YOU'LL NEED:

- A ladder towel rail. We got this one from IKEA, but lots of home stores have them. If you've already got one in your bathroom or bedroom, hijack it for the holidays and make this hack even cheaper!
- Mixture of foliage: faux + dried + real from the garden. We used dried palm leaves and pampas grass for their dramatic shape and interest.
- Plant ties and plastic ties – you'll need a few packets, as there's a lot going on here.
- Rope for hanging the ladder.

HERE'S HOW YOU DO IT:

- Lay the ladder flat on the ground.
- Tie the plants to one side of the ladder, starting with the largest and most architectural pieces of foliage.
- Keep going until you're happy with how it's looking and you can't see any of the ladder through the plants.
- Loop the rope around the ladder and then tie it securely – decorated side down – to the pergola, centred above the table.

Enjoy your meal underneath this glorious creation!

Hot tip

Pile crushed ice into a giant clamshell, and you've got yourself one stunning serving platter. Bring on the shellfish!

Space saver

To create more
space for feasting
on a small table, skip
the centrepiece and
hang your greenery
and lanterns above
the table.

SWEET AND SIMPLE MANTEL

This green garland is ridiculously easy to pull together and looks gorgeous on top of any mantelpiece.

YOU'LL NEED:

⭐ A decent amount of greenery – either real or fake.
⭐ Wire mesh cut into a long strip that is slightly narrower than the width of the mantelpiece.
⭐ Twist ties or plant ties.
⭐ A few white candles of varying heights (but see our warning on the opposite page!)

HERE'S HOW YOU DO IT:

⭐ Thread your greenery through the wire mesh, and secure it with the ties so you have a long runner of greenery.
⭐ Place the garland on the mantelpiece, and arrange the candles around it.

Drape the garland down the sides of the mantel for more drama!

SIMPLE STOCKINGS

This hack is such an easy way to give everyone a cute stocking that makes them feel special without ruining the colour scheme that you've worked hard to create. These ones look perfectly at home by this fireplace, and they only cost a few dollars each!

YOU'LL NEED:

⭐ Plain Christmas stockings from a craft store or discount department store.
⭐ Festive-looking letters and decorations such as stars.
⭐ Greenery from the garden – one sprig per stocking.
⭐ String.

HERE'S HOW YOU DO IT:

⭐ Tie a letter and/or decoration plus a sprig of greenery to each stocking with the string.
⭐ Hang the stockings from the mantelpiece.

Job done! Now that you've hung those stockings with care, it's time to put your feet up.

Christmas decorations don't need to be gaudy. Simplicity = stylish.

A word to the wise

The shorter candles are purely decorative. Don't light them unless you want an actual fire burning on top of the mantel.

#GRISWOLDS

EVER SEEN A WREATH SALAD BEFORE?

It's so simple and so effective. And would you believe us if we said that it even tastes better in this shape? #truestory

YOU HAD ME AT HELLO!

Welcome your guests with a pretty-as-a-picture mocktail. Bundaberg Pink Grapefruit (ginger beer) + pink fairy floss (cotton candy) + edible flowers = a mocktail you'll have to fight the kids for.

CUTE COUPE

We do love a coupe. These saucer-style glasses are perfectly suited to serving champers or cocktails, and we feel just a touch fancier drinking out of them, too. Ooh la la!

SHOWCASE THE HOLIDAY HERO

Why not turn the main element of the Christmas meal into a major moment? Spray a few palm fronds gold (dead easy), fan them out and then pop a few stems of pampas grass and fresh flowers in front of them to create a dramatic backdrop for your holiday ham. Drumroll please!

Star-shaped pillows match the twinkling stars above the bed and are a nod to Christmas.

SPRINKLE SOME HOLIDAY SPIRIT AROUND YOUR GUESTROOMS

Fresh white sheets and plenty of pillows are always a good place to start when styling a bedroom, but they also provide the perfect backdrop for a few festive touches. A gorgeous wreath (such as this Aussie twist on a traditional wreath), some twinkling stars and a basket of pressies (real or fake!) will have your guests dreaming of pavs and plum puddings in no time.

CREATING A CHRISTMAS VISION

For each of our projects – from a room restyle to a full-on rebuild – our first port of call is creating a vision board. Styling for Christmas is no different. For this 'summer in Australia' vibe, we pulled together pics and inspo for outdoor dining, native flora, natural colours and all things casual and relaxed. Only then did we start shopping and collecting styling items. What does your dream theme look like? #holidaysathome #staycation

WOW THE CROWD

Transform a corner of your yard into a glamping moment for a party like no other. A gorgeous canvas tent is an investment, but if you have to have one, then hop online and search for one that's large enough to host 'glampouts' and backyard parties (this one is 4.5 metres in diameter). Alternatively, you may be able to find party stores that rent them by the day for a fraction of the price of buying one. Once you've got that gorgeous tent up (and, before you ask, a boring one from the local camping store won't cut the mustard!), create a soft and luxurious foundation by layering rugs and cushions. Add a few low tables so guests have places to set down drinks and food, and then finish with some pretty touches: think fresh flowers, candles and greenery.

Blush puts a pretty spin on a Christmas theme.

Hot tip

String up some fairy lights, and place a few lanterns around the garden to turn this into an unforgettable evening under the stars. We hung a charming chandelier from the entrance here – it doesn't light up, but it does ensure that this tent is fit for a queen! #crowningglory

BONUS CHAPTER

Reno School
ROCK STARS

'BIRDS' IN THE WILD

When the three of us sat down to create our online course, The Reno School, our goal was to establish the ultimate reno resource – a course SO comprehensive and SO supportive that our students would be dripping in confidence by the end of it. There'd be no home project they couldn't tackle. We crammed every last tip, trick and hard-learned lesson into it. Basically, we made the course *we* wished we'd had at the beginning of our journey. And now, we get to watch as our students – reno rock stars in the making – flex their skills all over the world.

Every time we welcome a new intake of students, we get the biggest buzz because we know that our baby Reno School birds are mere weeks away from flying the nest and turning all of those lessons into real-life magic. You should hear us 'oohing' and 'aahing' whenever the latest batch of incredible transformations is shared with us. #soproud #passthekleenex

From forever homes to holiday rentals and brand new builds, our clever graduates are out in the world making magic happen. To us, this proves what we already knew: anyone can create their dream home with the right know-how, support and confidence.

On the following pages, we hand the mic over to some of our fabulously talented Reno School alumni so they can share their reno success stories.

TENNILLE HOLT

GOLD COAST, QLD, AUSTRALIA

My entire vision of a luxe resort feeling at home was based on this floating daybed.

In Tennille's words...

IT TAKES BLOOD, SWEAT AND $$$$ TO GET WHAT YOU WANT

I was heartbroken when my builders said this day bed couldn't be hung where I wanted it. Instead, they built a structure with oversized beams so they could hang the day bed in the open part of the deck. I hated it. Not only did it block our view, but it was also outside in the elements so there was major tannin staining, which meant that I was continually repainting that section of the deck. After further investigation, a good engineer, lots of cash and a NEW builder, we were able to move the day bed to my original spot. Since then, I have literally used it every day! It's completely under cover, so it's in the shade when it's sunny, and it's the perfect place to watch the show when a storm rolls in. This was a VERY expensive exercise but it was a lesson in following your gut and staying true to your original vision.

KEEP THOSE CLOTHES CONTAINED

For me, it was a MUST to have doors on the closet. I've lived in homes with walk-in robes that were all open, but I prefer not to see clothes on display. Doors keep everything looking beautiful at all times.

GET YOUR GLAM ON

I highly recommend creating a 'glam nook' somewhere in your closet so you have a place to store all of your make-up and hair tools, and get ready in good lighting.

Shower hobs are the BEST! I recommend them 100 per cent, as they help to keep the water in the shower area.

Wondering what the outside of Tennille's home looks like? Turn back to the previous spread.

DEBBIE WONG

NOOSA, QLD, AUSTRALIA

BEFORE

In Debbie's words...

RENO WITHOUT GOING FULL DEMO

Creating large openings in a wall can be a great compromise if the wall is structural but you love the open-plan look. By opening the wall between the kitchen and living area rather than knocking it out completely, we were able to provide a seamless connection between the two spaces without the cost or engineering headaches.

FROM OH-NO TO OH-WHOA!

Original plans don't always work out. When it became clear that lowering the living-room level to match the dining room was outside our budget, we got creative. By using a custom oak finish on the stairs that continued into the built-in bench seats for the dining table, we were able to use these split levels to our advantage. Now they're a stand-out feature.

Retaining some of the character from the original house adds to the story of a home. We saved these huge wooden beams (which were once part of Tasmanian wharfs and wartime Canadian boats), and made them a feature. Now they give the space both character and warmth, and soften the architecture of the home.

WHAT YOU SEE IS WHAT YOU GET

Choosing exterior finishes is a big responsibility. These are costly decisions, and you don't want to get them wrong. We found that using computer-generated 3D rendering helped us visualise how things would look and allowed us to make decisions we would be happy with.

LOW-MAINTENANCE MATERIALS ARE YOUR FRIEND

It's important to consider the ongoing maintenance costs of any materials you use, but that's especially true when it comes to your home's exterior. I wanted to use timber battens for the privacy screens, but they were going to be too costly to maintain due to our coastal location, so metal won out.

Choose interior finishes and furniture that pick up on the surrounding views. Here, timber, organic shapes and earthy tones echo the materials of Noosa National Park.

HANNAH SILVERTON

BANGALOW, NSW, AUSTRALIA

My plumber bent a plain old length of copper pipe around the tyre of his ute to get the perfect curve for my copper shower.

In Hannah's words...

ASK ABOUT 'EARTHING'

In Australia, pool fences with metal elements such as spigots or handrails have to be built more than 1.25 metres away from a pool so people in the water can't reach over and electrocute themselves. We didn't learn this until it was too late. Our concrete pool tiles and fence were installed quite close to the water, so we had to have the tiles pulled up so an electrician could 'earth' the spigots (diverting any future electric current to the ground and thereby preventing electric shock). If we hadn't done this, we would have had to put plastic casings over each of the metal spigots.

DON'T LEAVE THIS TIL LAST

If an outdoor shower is in the stars for you, map out its exact location early on in the process so the plumbing for that shower (including whether you want hot and cold water) can be tackled *before* any concrete or decking goes down.

SEAMLESS BATTENS

Timber-batten fences like this one really suit a natural setting, but be sure to ask your landscaper to screw the battens onto the posts from the *back* of the fence rather than the front. That way, you get a beautiful seamless fence with no visible screws.

PROTECT YOUR POOL

An integrated, automated pool cover is a must when locating your pool near established trees. Not only is it good from a heating and safety point of view, but it also keeps leaves, fruit, bird and bat droppings and branches out of the water. We didn't plan for this in our budget, and our builders told us a cover wasn't necessary, but now that I spend so much time and money on pool maintenance, I wish we'd added it.

221

EMMA RAMIA

TOOWOOMBA, QLD,
AUSTRALIA

BEFORE

In Emma's words...

UNLOCK THE CHARM

Ripping down an awkward addition can be the fastest way to uncover an old home's character. Taking away the sunroom at the front of this house changed so much: we gained more storage space in the front bedroom and were able to add a pretty verandah under the existing roofline. The gorgeous front window, which had been hiding behind that sunroom for decades, was finally on show again.

KNOW WHAT YOUR BUYERS ARE INTO

We knew that buyers of old cottages in our area love original flooring, so rather than replace the hardwood floors, we sanded them back and gave them a coat of clear varnish (not too glossy). The floors came up great, and the money we saved meant that we could spend a little more on the kitchen's stone benchtop.

Fretwork doesn't have to be expensive or overly ornate. I showed our builder a picture I found on Pinterest, and he knocked up this fretwork in no time at all.

AIMEE M^cKECHNIE

GERRINGONG, NSW, AUSTRALIA

In Aimee's words...

DECISIONS, DECISIONS

When your dining table sits next to the kitchen island, you have a choice to make because hanging pendants over both will create a visual fight. We went with pendants over the dining table and three canister lights above the island. Canister lights are economical, and also have those clean modern lines we like. Choosing white for both sets of lights helps them to visually connect, without clashing.

WOOD LOOK, FOR LESS

If you want wooden joinery but don't have the budget for wood veneer or solid wood, European laminate is a wonderful option. It's a little bit more expensive than regular laminate but really looks like solid wood.

SOFT, SIMPLE SHEERS

Oatmeal-coloured sheer curtains are a great alternative to white if you're after an earthy, natural feeling. These ones offer a 'linen look' but are much cheaper than the real deal, and you'd never guess that they weren't real linen just from looking at them.

COASTAL COLOURS GET THE HEAVE-HO

Even though this holiday rental is a beach house, I wanted soft, warm tones and a minimal look rather than the blues and greys you often find in coastal homes. The pinky linen chairs (the colour is called 'Piglet', if you're wondering), creams and wood tones create a feeling that is cosy and welcoming. We wanted people to be able to walk into this space, flop into a chair and feel super comfortable.

We went with small Australian designers for all of the furniture. It's great to support local designers if you can.

Placing a substantial plant outside a window can turn a 'meh' view into a calming palm-scape.

SWAP TV FOR BOARD GAMES

You won't find a TV in this lounge room because we didn't want it competing for attention. The idea was to encourage people to carry their conversation from the dining table into the lounge area. After all, holidays are about connecting and creating memories. This plan worked – I often get tagged in photos of guests playing board games and enjoying lazy evenings here.

TEXTURES CREATE A FEATURE

If a room is lacking the X-factor, adding a floor-to-ceiling reclaimed brick wall around a fireplace creates a real focal point. These bricks were cheaper than standard house bricks, and the mortar between them was scraped out a bit to give the wall some definition. Adding this feature was an extra cost, but it was less expensive than using cladding or stone around the fireplace.

The front door of this home is featured on page 213.

CHRISSY LEWRY

MACMASTERS BEACH, NSW, AUSTRALIA

In Chrissy's words ...

HIDE THE POOL ACCESSORIES

Keep in mind that pools come with pumps and lots of other equipment. Plan ahead so they can be hidden out of sight. You don't want those items ruining the view. We built a room under the cabana for this exact reason.

PAY FOR A DECENT POOL TILER

This is not an area in which you should try to save money. My pool tiler pointed out how bad it looks when pool tiles aren't laid well or joined perfectly, and he was right – it throws the whole pool off. A good pool tiler is worth every cent.

I always include room for a stool or two on the cook's side of the island, so I can sit with my guests while I'm chopping or stirring.

PLAN EARLY FOR ANY WOW FEATURES

At the framing stage, talk to your tradespeople about any big decorative features you are planning to use, so they can advise you about what's needed to support them. The cloud light here required five rows of treated pine pieces in the ceiling space to support its weight. We made them a little longer than they needed to be so I had some flexibility with position when the time came to hang the light.

GET VOCAL ON VEIN SELECTION

Once you find a slab of stone you love for your island, tell the stonecutters which veins you like (or which ones you don't), so that when the slab shows up on site, it's been cut to showcase the most beautiful veins.

My home feels like a holiday.
#STAYCATION

Hot tip

Visit a factory that sells stone or marble and ask to see their offcuts. The gorgeous offcuts can be glued onto plain bathroom vanities, transforming them into something that looks truly high-end.

DEB McNEE

BALGOWLAH, NSW,
AUSTRALIA

In Deb's words...

PLAY WITH PRINT IN A POWDER ROOM

Black herringbone tiles and a black vanity make this bold print stand out even more, and give this room a luxe-hotel vibe. When the door is left open, the view into the room is like a piece of art in itself.

WALLPAPERING? BUY MORE THAN YOU NEED

The guy doing our wallpaper ran out of paper by literally half a drop due to the pattern and the way it was cut! He couldn't come back to finish the job, which meant that I had to upskill and do it myself. #canyoutell?

STICK TO YOUR VISION

I tend to love everything and can be easily thrown off track once I click on Pinterest or Instagram. But sticking to the style and theme of your original vision boards really does make the whole process so much smoother. The Reno School course cemented this for me.

Installing tapware to the side of a sink rather than behind it shows off its gorgeous shape and adds interest.

PUT SOME TECH IN YOUR OUTDOOR CEILING

Roof tech takes this whole outdoor area to the next level. We can play music outside and still watch sport on TV inside, have the fans going when it's warmer in summer and flick the heaters on in winter. It's bliss!

OUTDOOR SKYLIGHTS ARE A THING

When your roofline extends out, skylights ensure that the inside of the house still gets plenty of natural light. You don't need fancy skylights, either. These ones are standard glass panels that simply slot between the beams.

SPLIT UP POOL JOBS TO SAVE MONEY

The cost of a pool can be reduced if you're willing to split that project into stages. We employed a separate excavation company and a stand-alone pool builder, and then we hired building contractors to get the retaining walls done. This meant that we were able to see how much we were spending on each stage and negotiate the price rather than having it all bundled into one large project. There was more admin work, but the savings were worth it.

JULIE GRANGER

BINNA BURRA, NSW, AUSTRALIA

In Julie's words...

TAKE GOOD NOTES, AND THEN KEEP THEM SOMEWHERE SAFE

If you meet with a builder or other tradesperson on site to agree to the position of something, be sure to write down whatever has been agreed to and take photos. We spent an hour in this kitchen working out the pendant placement with our electrician and then we returned home – 800 kilometres away. Turned out he had written our agreed measurements down ... right on top of the kitchen island before the stone benchtop went on! We had to have the whole meeting again over FaceTime, which wasn't the same.

ISLANDS CAN WORK IN NARROW KITCHENS

Placing a dominant island bench in a narrow space may not be for everyone, but if entertaining is important to you, it could be the right way to go. We managed to squeeze this island in with enough space to move on either side, and we created room at the end of the island for up to five people to sit.

SEE SOMETHING YOU LOVE? BUY IT!

If you have a clear vision for your renovation and you stumble across something in a sale that ties in with that, grab it! I bought these kitchen pendants long before this renovation began and have no regrets.

STITCH THE FLOORS TOGETHER

In old houses, removing walls to make spaces bigger often creates issues with original wooden floors. When we removed a bathroom to make this kitchen bigger, the bathroom floorboards were running in a different direction to those in the kitchen. If keeping the original floors is a priority for you, ask the builder to pull up those boards and then 'stitch' them in with the other floorboards so they all run in the same direction. It is time-consuming, but we reckon the end result is well worth it.

GIVE YOUR POOL THE BEST OUTLOOK

If you want to showcase a view but your vision board calls for a timber fence rather than a glass fence, why not dip the fence? The height of this fence drops by about a metre right in front of the pool, making it low enough to reveal the bush beyond, but high enough to comply with safety regulations.

ARE YOU READY TO TAKE THE PLUNGE?

Installing a prefab concrete plunge pool added so much value to our Airbnb. It was delivered pre-tiled, ready to be dropped into place and plumbed in. And our guests really love it!

LAUREN CECIL

GOLD COAST, QLD, AUSTRALIA

In Lauren's words ...

KEEP REFINING YOUR STYLE UNTIL IT BECOMES CLEAR

If you haven't nailed your style yet, don't stop looking until you land on something that feels right. I was torn between two styles: my barn-style vision board was moody and very 'country', while my coastal vision board was really light and airy. I loved both styles but didn't know how to bring them together ... until I saw Bonnie's home. Seeing how she had executed a barn and coastal style gave me confidence that I could bring the two styles together, and I never looked back.

SCALE IN THE SPOTLIGHT

If the height of a room is really grand, you don't need to go overboard with furnishings and finishes. Keeping the other details minimal draws attention to that wow factor.

INTERNAL WINDOWS CAN BE GAME-CHANGING

Adding internal windows to a long hallway can turn it from a gloomy corridor to a light-filled runway. These internal windows were a last-minute addition (inspired by the Birds, see page 21), but they turned out to be one of the best things I did. The light they grab keeps the hallway feeling bright and open, and the windows themselves are an appealing feature to look at when you're sitting in the living room.

I love the way this tall pot filled with bamboo sticks draws the eye up to the exposed rafters.

Malawi-look chairs around this concrete table add texture and warmth.

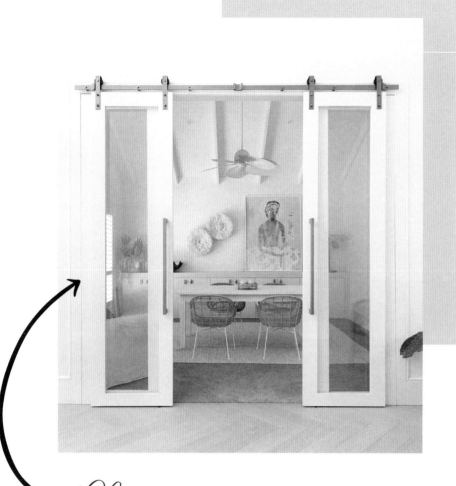

Office inspo

The built-ins, chunky benchtop and barn doors are all inspired by Sophie's house (yep, that's the Three Birds' home on pages 40–79)!

Hot tip

These glass barn doors were on the more expensive side, but we saved money by buying a couple of standard tracks from Bunnings, welding them together and then powder coating them in brass for a bespoke look.

YOU CAN PAINT NEW FURNITURE, TOO

I bought a new table for this office. Its size and style were right for the space, but the soft salmon colour just wasn't working. In the end, I took some leftover white paint from the exterior of our house and went for it! I love how it turned out.

CREATE A SEAMLESS LINK BETWEEN KITCHENS

By using the same stone benchtop inside and outside, the same tapware and the same style of cabinetry, we created a seamless link between the kitchen and the alfresco kitchenette. Be sure to check that the stone you're going to use on any benchtop outside will be okay in the sun. I asked this question early on and chose a stone that could be used in both areas.

LAST-MINUTE CHANGES HAVE THEIR PLACE

No matter how much you plan your renovation or build, there are bound to be moments where you stand in a space as it's coming together and think, *You know what, this isn't going to work.* That's just part of the process. The roof over this alfresco area was one of those moments. It was going to be flat, but once the frames went up, we decided to continue the cathedral-style roofline from inside through to the outside to allow a lot more light inside.

A well-stocked outdoor bar fridge keeps adults and kids out of the main kitchen and frees up fridge space for food.

LUCY MILLER

GEELONG, VIC, AUSTRALIA

In Lucy's words...

IT'S NEVER TOO LATE TO ADD MORE LIGHT

If you realise that a room – especially a kitchen – is going to be too dark, and you are able to stretch the budget, I don't think you'll ever regret putting in a skylight or two. These two were a late addition to our plans, but we're so glad we have them. They make this kitchen sparkle.

★ **DIY HACK** ★

Upcycled stools

I found these stools on Gumtree for a bargain price, painted them off-white to match the island cabinets, then got handy with a staple gun and some pretty fabric to create the chair pads.

Don't like your staircase's dodgy old handrail? Replace it with a timber-batten wall for a statement look.

SOFA RESCUE

Quite often, all a couch needs is a new cover to see it through the next era of its life. This 20-year-old couch had great bones, so we changed the cushion fillings from foam to feather to give it a more contemporary feel, and then we re-covered it. When I couldn't find a pinstripe linen fabric I liked in any stores, I bought two king-size doona covers made from linen and had them made into slip covers. Yes, I got a few funny looks from the seamstress, but they look beautiful *and* they're washable.

SHELVES FOR SMALL THINGS

If space is tight around a front door or staircase, a discreet shelf can be the neatest (and cheapest) solution. We added a little shelf at the bottom of the stairs and painted it, and it does a great job of holding keys and mail.

TIFFANY CAMPBELL

IPSWICH, QLD, AUSTRALIA

Buy a jar from Kmart for less than $3, saw the lid in half and screw your two half-moon handles into place.

In Tiffany's words...

MAJOR MARBLE HACK

If you want a marble benchtop but cash is tight, this might be the tip for you. This benchtop is actually made of fibre-cement sheeting, which is a concrete grey colour. When I really wanted whiter-looking benchtops, a friend of ours who is a renderer suggested that I try using white oxide over feather coat (also called feather finish) – a cement-based smoothing compound. While I was applying the oxide on top, I noticed that it wasn't mixing properly with the feather coat – it was creating veining and movement like marble. So I applied three coats of feather coat and oxide, drying and sanding in between each coat, and then sealed the benchtop with a waterproof sealant. All up, this DIY project cost us $300. We've had small kids who spilled stuff on the benchtop, but we never had an issue. I'd do this again in a heartbeat over spending $20,000 on marble.

BARN DOOR BLISS

This old barn door came from a previous renovation. We sanded it back, put a clear coat of varnish on it, and it turned out to be the quirky rustic touch this kitchen needed.

NYOME BLANCHARD

FERN BAY, NSW, AUSTRALIA

In Nyome's words...

STEAL SLICES OF LIGHT

If you don't want the neighbours seeing into your kitchen, but you want more natural light, consider building a long window across the top of a wall. The window above our upper cabinets gives us light from every angle no matter the time of day, and it makes the space feel bright and private.

CAN'T GO WRONG WITH A CURVE

Adding a curve to this island and to the back appliance wall made this room so much better. We changed the kitchen plans to add these details, and I've never regretted it. This is the one thing that everyone comments on and touches when they walk past. Without these curves, this would be a harsh space. Instead, it strikes the right balance between minimalist and comfort.

SHEER DELIGHT

This kitchen wouldn't be the same without these sheer curtains. They are purely for look and feel, not privacy. Once I knew I wanted them, I made space in the budget for them and made compromises elsewhere to ensure we could afford them. The length we needed wasn't available on the company's website, but I picked up the phone and asked if they could make them longer to fit our high ceilings, and they were happy to make them for us. Always ask the question.

STALK THE SALES

It's so much easier to fit a new kitchen around appliances than it is to plan a new kitchen and then find appliances to fit. Months before our build began, we bought two ovens, a microwave and a coffee machine on sale. Having these appliances early helped us create symmetry in our kitchen design, because we were able to work our cabinets around them.

239

KATY SCHUMAN

PARADISE VALLEY, AZ,
UNITED STATES

In Katy's words …

INSPO VIA IBIZA

This design was based on an image of an old house in Ibiza. We took elements from that picture – like the recessed cabinetry – and refined them for a less rustic look. Achieving this look was more tedious than a standard build, because everything had to be fitted perfectly. The cavities had to be framed up and plastered, and then the appliances and cabinets had to slot neatly inside them without any big gaps. Even though our builders had done inset work before, they weren't used to this recessed style. I wanted everything sitting flush, because I felt that this seamless look was the key to this kitchen. Even though I had to compromise and have some things sitting a little prouder, the end result still gives us the feeling of that Ibiza home.

YOU CAN TWEAK YOUR TIMBER TONE

We chose a white French oak timber for the kitchen cabinets, but it had yellow and pink tones that didn't work with the look we wanted. After our cabinet-makers bleached it for us, we had the perfect shade of blond timber to work with. It pays to ask which treatments are available so you get the exact shade you're after.

Three Birds Renovations has been a big influence on my style. I just added a few of my own flairs.

I didn't want to ruin the lines of the cross-vault ceiling by installing lots of downlights, so the plasterer formed built-in plaster sconces in each corner. Now, when the lights are on, they highlight the beautiful arches and make them even more of a feature.

We recessed the wooden headers to link them back to the recessed timber cabinets in the kitchen. We also added a secret pocket behind them to hide the blackout shade.

WEATHERED WOOD IS A GREAT MIDDLE GROUND

We wanted to add timber beams to this room, but new timber didn't have enough character, and reclaimed beams had too much. They were just a little too beat up and rustic for this new build. Instead, we went with weathered wood, which is timber that has been exposed to the elements but not used. It has character, but is a little more refined than reclaimed wood.

WELL-TRAVELLED PIECES CAN MAKE A ROOM

The furniture here comes from all over the world: the rug is Moroccan, the bench at the end of the bed is from India, the bed is from Bali and the plaster side tables were custom made. But they all share the same colour palette, so their textures and styles don't feel out of place next to each other.

BELGIAN BLUESTONE CRUSH

Belgian bluestone is a timeless limestone – it was used for a lot of cobblestone streets in Europe. These floor tiles were more expensive than other options (especially since we ended up airfreighting them from Europe). But I love their soft charcoal black against the white plaster and wood tones in the house. Belgian bluestone feels nice to walk on, is super easy to care for and looks better the older it gets. You might freak out about the first scratch when it's new, but it develops a patina that is really beautiful the more worn it gets. And with three kids and three dogs, that was a selling point!

These sleek chairs play well with the more traditional-looking fireplace.

WARM UP YOUR FIREPLACE

We used reclaimed firebricks for the inside of our fireplace, because we loved the way these old bricks warm up this room. Reclaimed firebricks are pricey, but they're a nice touch for a little fireplace like this.

See how this space connects with the kitchen on page 212.

245

SET THE SCENE WITH ESTABLISHED TREES

Planting an established tree or two at the front of a new build instantly anchors it in that location and makes it look like it's been there for much longer. We chose these two 150-year-old olive trees because they suited the Spanish style of our home perfectly. They were expensive to buy and plant, but the sense of place and history they add completely changes the feeling of the house.

BUT WAIT, THERE'S MORE!

If you enjoyed this book, you're going to *love* our online Reno School and Three Birds Styling School.

The Reno School and Styling School are online courses created by us to teach you everything we know about how to design, renovate (or build) and style your dream home. We'll help you create a vision for your project, understand who you need to work with, how to handle tradies, manage a budget and style a space. We'll show you where to spend versus where to save, and how to avoid basic mistakes that can chew up your time, money and happy reno vibes. In a nutshell, these courses are a much more detailed version of this book, with ten times the content!

Whether you're renovating, doing a new build or simply styling a space, you need vision and know-how to get what you want. Our Reno School and Styling School will fast-track your knowledge, build your confidence and get you ready to reno, build and style!

Join the tens of thousands of students who have already completed our courses and get 10% off with this exclusive discount code – IBOUGHTYOURBOOK

Are you ready to make your dream home a reality?

Visit threebirdsrenovations.com today!

INDEX

A

additions 37, 222
arches 19, 49, 56, 112, 113, 114
armchairs, in bathrooms 170
artwork
   complementing hues with
     128
   diversity in 98
   height of 113, 181
   in bedrooms 166, 167
   in offices 182, 185, 186
   matching colour palettes 15
   mirrors as 116
   neutral backgrounds for 20
   placement of 160
   prints 57
   to reflect the setting 156
asymmetry 113
Australian Staycation 136–81
awnings, motorised 95

B

balustrades 74, 75
bar carts 78
bathrooms
   bi-folds for open-air bathing
     65
   black sink and vanity 93, 94
   choosing fixtures 64
   costing fixtures 64
   gold taps and sconces 93
   herringbone tiles 98
   mirrored cabinets 95
   shower-over-bath set-up 27
   tiling in 27
   using repetition in design 70
   walk-around baths 170

bathtubs 27
bedrooms
   bedheads 66, 67, 129, 180
   built-in beds 66–7
   built-in bunks 24, 25
   cosmetic renovations 28
   half-pipe beds 118, 119
   in beige 180
   lighting in 92
   plants in 57
   timber beams in 244
bedside tables 29
Belgian bluestone 245
Bell, Sophie 42, 47, 69, 74
bench seats 18, 19, 31, 55, 59,
    111, 114–15, 159
benchtops 30, 31, 50, 109, 160,
    234, 238
besser blocks 133
bi-folds 25, 29, 64, 65, 153
Blanchard, Nyome 239
blinds 72, 113, 116–17
board-and-batten walls 141
The Bold Extension 80–101
breakfast nooks 54
breeze blocks 133
brick pavers 133
bricks, reclaimed 225, 245
bunks 24, 25
butler's pantries 161

C

Campbell, Tiffany 238
Cape Cod house 12
carpets 28
Cecil, Lauren 232
ceiling fans 152

ceilings
   cross-vault ceilings 242
   feature ceilings 22, 174–5
   high ceilings 232
   outdoor ceilings 229
   raked ceilings 86, 87, 161
   wallpaper on 118, 119
chairs 34, 35, 112, 159, 160
chandeliers 90, 171, 186, 211
children's rooms 72, 118, 173
Christmas decorations 197, 198,
    201, 204–7
Christmas with the Birds 194–211
cladding 106, 135, 141, 157
colour
   connecting space with 112
   contrasts of 141
   feature colours on ceilings 174–5
   gold trim 106
   in children's rooms 72
   neutral tones 86
   of artworks 15, 54, 55
   reversing colour schemes 22
   stripes and blue tones 15
   using beige 180
   using black 85, 93–5, 151
   using bold colours 118
   using green 48, 88
   using grey 125
   using one colour to create cohesion
    37, 164
   using pink 25, 188, 225
   using timeless colours 173
   using white 28, 48, 66, 67, 86, 151,
    170, 199
Colour Me Hamptons 10–39
company signs 190

Contemporary Cottage 102–35
costs 64, 123, 220, 229
couches 59
coupes 208
crosshatching 24, 31, 34
curtains 113, 146–7, 224, 239
cushions 15, 39, 115, 133
cutlery 199

D
day beds 16, 78, 154, 155, 216
dining rooms 32–3, 54, 55, 90, 159,
    243, 245
dishwashers 110
doors
    barn doors 238
    bi-fold shutter doors 25, 29
    French glass doors 145
    glass barn-door sliders 60, 234
    opening on to porches 152, 153
    sliding doors 151, 234
drinks trolleys 78
dryers 162
Dulux 25, 85, 107, 118, 180, 188

E
earthing, of spigots 221
ensuites 127, 170–1, 176
entertaining 58–9, 79, 211
extensions 37, 80–101

F
facade facelifts 84
feminine and masculine balance
    166–7
fencing 150, 221, 231
fireplaces 116, 207, 245

flooring
    chequerboard floors 140, 141
    engineered timber 115
    floorboards with rugs 166
    hardwood floors 222
    herringbone and chevron patterns
       161
    in front entries 19
    mismatches after removing walls 230
    timber flooring 59
floral arrangements 204
fretwork 106, 223
fridges 50, 52
front entries 19, 106, 145
front-loading washing machines 26,
    27, 62

G
garden sheds 134, 135
giant clamshells 85, 204
glass display cases 86
glass, noise-reducing 90
gold trim 106
Granger, Julie 230
grouting 123

H
handles 162, 191, 238
HardieDeck 132
Holt, Tennille 216
home offices 56

I
ice buckets 203

J
juju hats 116

K
kitchen appliances 239
kitchens
    cabinetry 86, 87, 161, 240–1
    concrete look 52
    glass display cases 86
    in offices 191
    island benches 50–1, 88–9, 109,
       156, 160, 227, 230
    mixing styles 88
    open-plan layouts 50–1
    timber kitchens 108–9
    walkways in 110
    white kitchens 86

L
laminate 224
landscaping 36
laundries 26–7, 62, 63, 110, 162
Lewry, Chrissy 226
lighting
    canister lights 224
    carriage lights 92
    cloud lights 227
    floor lamps 192
    in bedrooms 92
    in outdoor areas 78
    pendants 30–1, 50, 61, 112, 145,
       154–5, 160, 190, 224
living rooms 58–9, 158, 159, 218–19,
    242

M
marble 227
masculine and feminine balance
    166–7
mattresses 119

McKechnie, Aimee 224
McNee, Deb 228
Mediterranean Farmhouse 40–79
microcement 124
Miller, Lucy 236
mirrors 98, 111, 116
mocktails 208

N
natural light 56, 62, 64, 95, 130, 161, 236, 239
new houses 46
NRG Greenboard 74

O
offices 56, 182–93
optical illusions 145
outdoor areas 34, 35, 36–9, 61, 78–9, 132

P
painting 152, 156, 188, 191, 234
panelling 92
pavers 74, 75, 133
pearlescent paint 156
pedestal basins 178
pendants 30–1, 50, 61, 112, 145, 154–5, 160, 190, 224
pergolas 98–9, 130, 131
pillows 210
plants
  banana palms 106
  Bangalow palms 141
  cycad palms 141
  fake pot plants 21
  hanging plants 205
  in sightlines 225
  indoors 147
  mixing real and faux plants 200
  olive trees 246–7
  pygmy palms 158
  raffia palms 141
  to add height and colour 181
  using established plants 141, 246–7
  vertical gardens 123
plunge pools 231
pots 18, 19, 85, 106, 135, 145
powder rooms 26–7, 228
power points 29, 187
privacy screens 84, 220

R
Ramia, Emma 213, 222
rendering 74
The Reno School and Styling School 214, 249
Reno School Rock Stars 212–47
roof spaces 178–9
roof tiles 34, 140, 141
rugs 159, 165, 173

S
Schuman, Katy 212, 240
sconces 242
second-storey additions 37
shaving cabinets 98, 176
sheds 134, 135
shelves 237
showers
  copper showers 221
  mixers in 126, 127
  open showers 124–5
  outdoor showers 74, 221
  shower hobs 217
  shower niches 64
  shower screens 126, 127
  showerheads 125, 126
  windows in 156, 157
  with finger tiles 176, 177
shutters 34
sideboards 98–9, 181
Silverton, Hannah 221
sinks 31
skirting boards 26, 174
skylights 229, 236
sofas 58–9, 186, 237
souvenirs 164, 165, 244
spaces, connection of 112
spigots 150, 221
splashbacks 52
spritz sheds 134, 135
stairs 18, 237
stone 52, 227
stools 145, 236
storage 16, 18, 118, 119, 163, 193
stripes 173
styling
  using curves 15, 116, 123, 132–3, 164, 239
  using lines 84
  using repetition 70, 164
  using shape 62
swimming pools 36–7, 76–7, 150, 221, 226, 229, 231
symmetry 141, 146–7

T
table settings 199, 200, 202–3
tables 72, 144, 190, 233, 243, 245

tapware
 brass tapware 64
 bronze tapware 124, 125
 chrome tapware 29
 gold tapware 93, 164, 165, 170
 in laundries 62, 63
Three Birds HQ 182–93

tiling
 Belgian bluestone tiles 245
 bold floor tiles 95
 diamond patterns 156, 157
 doubling the grout lines 123
 encaustic-look floor tiles 95
 finger tiles 176, 177
 herringbone patterns 98, 228
 in bathrooms 27
 in front entries 19, 106
 in outdoor areas 34
 indoors to outdoors 142–3
 roof tiles 34
 swimming pools 226
timber battens 120, 237
timber bump outs 107
toilets 95, 125, 176
turf 130, 131, 149

V
vanities 65, 70, 93, 123, 164, 165,
  228
vases 98, 187
verandahs 84
vertical gardens 123

W
wall cavities 22
wall vinyl 165
wallpaper 23, 96, 118, 119, 228

walls
 adding interest to white walls 54
 board-and-batten walls 141
 creating openings in 218–19
 floating vanity walls 170, 171
 modular walls 38–9
 reclaimed brick walls 225
 removing 230
 removing load-bearing walls 114
 timber mouldings on 186
 transition walls 127
wardrobes 68–9, 128, 168, 169, 217
washing machines 26, 27, 62, 162
window trims 106

windows
 bi-fold windows 64, 65, 153
 for privacy 239
 framing a view 90
 gas-strut windows 154, 155
 in new homes 46
 in showers 156, 157
 internal windows 232
 splashbacks 52
wonder walls 21
Wong, Debbie 218
wreaths 198, 208, 210

Z
zones 36, 187

THANK YOU

Our first thank you must go to Jane Morrow at Murdoch Books. It took us a long time to decide whether or not to go again with a second book, and we wouldn't have said 'yes' if it weren't for your patience and understanding. Thank you for waiting.

And thank you to Virginia Birch and the whole crew at Murdoch Books – we feel the love, and you make publishing a book as easy as possible (not that it's easy!).

A very special thank you to Katie Bosher for helping to write the words. We couldn't have done it without you. You truly were the fourth Bird on this project, and we loved watching you and Lana debate the spelling of 'checkerboard' vs 'chequerboard'. #wordnerds

Jacqui Porter, we love the way you design our books. Thank you for bringing our vision to life and always being open to our creative input. And thank you to Megan Pigott for your attention to detail with our vision right to the end.

To our legendary photographers – Chris Warnes, Maree Homer, Jacqui Turk, Monique Easton, River Bennett, Jessie Prince and Hannah Blackmore – your stunning pics capture our homes in their best light, and this book showcases just how good you are.

To our Reno School students – we love seeing your reno progress and hearing your stories. Special shout-out to those few we were able to feature in this book. Your projects are proof of what's possible, and we couldn't be prouder of what our Reno Schoolers continue to achieve every day.

Hugs and kisses to our beautiful birdies who work with us daily in the nest – you're the support system we need to be able to write books like this one. You keep our world turning.

To you, our readers – thank you for coming on this journey and for making our first book such a success. We now know that it wasn't just our mums buying all of the copies. This second book was written for YOU – to help YOU create your dream home. Thank you for trusting us.

And finally, to our families – your love is our fuel.

Bonnie, Erin and Lana xxx

On-site is our happy place!

Published in 2021 by Murdoch Books, an imprint of Allen & Unwin

Murdoch Books Australia
83 Alexander Street
Crows Nest NSW 2065
Phone: +61 (0)2 8425 0100
murdochbooks.com.au
info@murdochbooks.com.au

Murdoch Books UK
Ormond House
26–27 Boswell Street
London WC1N 3JZ
Phone: +44 (0) 20 8785 5995
murdochbooks.co.uk
info@murdochbooks.co.uk

For corporate orders and custom publishing, contact our business development team at
salesenquiries@murdochbooks.com.au

Publisher: Jane Morrow
Creative direction: northwoodgreen.com
Manuscript collaboration: Katie Bosher
Editorial Manager: Virginia Birch
Editor: Dannielle Viera
Principal photographer: Chris Warnes
Illustrator: Sophie Bell
Production Director: Lou Playfair

Text © Three Birds Renovations 2021
The moral right of the author has been asserted.
Design © Murdoch Books 2021
Photography © Three Birds Renovations 2021,
except for Reno School Rock Stars (see below)

Photographs: 7, 106(b), 125, 128(b), 255(t), 255(bl), 255(br) by River Bennett © River Bennett; 248(br) by Hannah Blackmore © Hannah Blackmore; 5(tr), 5(bl), 21(b), 26, 34(b), 83(t), 90(b), 101, 182, 183, 184–5, 186, 187, 188–9, 190, 191, 192, 193(t), 193(b), 194, 195, 197, 198, 199(t), 199(b), 200, 201(l), 202–3, 204(t), 204(b), 207, 208(t), 208(b), 209, 210, 211, 248(bl) by Monique Easton © Monique Easton; front cover, back flap and pages 4(tl), 4(br), 5(tl), 10, 13(b), 14–15, 16, 18(t), 19(b), 32–3, 48–9, 59, 65, 66, 90(t), 96, 103, 107, 112–13, 115, 124, 132(t), 136, 137, 138–9, 142–3, 144, 145, 146–7, 154–5, 157, 159, 162(t), 164, 165, 169(l), 170–1, 172–3, 174–5, 178, 178–9, 188, 248(t) by Maree Homer © Maree Homer; 40, 49, 52, 54, 61(r), 78(b) by Jessie Prince © Jessie Prince; 161(l), 162(b), 168, 170, 176(r) by Jacqui Turk © Jacqui Turk; front flap, back cover (tr, mr, br) and pages 2–3, 4(tr), 4(bl), 11, 16–17, 18(b), 20, 21(t), 22(t), 23, 24, 25, 27, 28, 29(l), 29(r), 30, 31(l), 31(r), 34(t), 35, 36–7, 38–9, 39, 41, 43(r), 44–5, 46–7, 50–1, 53, 55, 56, 57, 58–9, 60, 61(l), 62, 63, 64, 66–7, 68, 70–1, 72, 73, 74, 75, 76–7, 78(t), 79, 80, 81, 83(b), 84, 85, 86(l), 86(r), 87, 88, 88–9, 91, 92(t), 92(r), 96–7, 98, 99, 102, 105(b), 108–9, 110(l), 110(r), 111, 114, 116–17, 118, 119, 120–1, 122, 123(l), 123(r), 126, 127, 128(t), 129, 130–1, 132(b), 133, 134, 135(l), 135(r), 140–1, 148–9, 150, 151(t), 151(b), 152, 153(t), 153(b), 156, 158, 160, 161(r), 163, 166, 167, 169(r), 176(l), 177, 180, 181, 201(r), 205 by Chris Warnes © Chris Warnes.

Reno School Rock Stars photographs: 233 © Adore Home Magazine; 218–19 © Aimee Dodge Photography; 235 © @andreavanheerden.creative for @uniqwacollections; 239(l), 239(r) © Nyome Blanchard; 238 © Tiffany Campbell; 232 © Lauren Cecil; 236, 237 © Rochelle Eagle for Adore Home Magazine; 222–3 © Fleur & Mae Photography; 214–15, 216, 217(l), 217(r) © Tennille Holt; 221(l), 221(r) © Anna Hutchcroft; 230, 231 © Morgan Kelly; 226 © Chrissy Lewry; 222 © Raine & Horne Toowoomba; 5(br), 212, 240–1, 242, 243, 244, 245, 246–7 © Werner Segarra; 227 © @shutterprojectaustralia; 213, 220(t), 220(b), 224, 225(l), 225(r) © Nat Spadavecchia @ The Palm Co; 234 © Villa Styling; 228, 229 © Helen Ward @ Inward Outward Photography; 218 © Debbie Wong.

Murdoch Books wishes to thank the following artists, photographers and suppliers, whose work appears in this book: 3, 144, 147 & 173 Kerrie Jeffs; 10, 14 & 19 DanielleX; 20 & 57 Slim Aarons supplied by Sunday Society and Fine Print Co.; 20 & 25 nature prints supplied by Designer Boys Art; 22 print supplied by Olive and Oriel; 22 & 97 neon signs supplied by Electric Confetti; 48 & 49 umbrella print by Stuart Cantor; 49 boat print by Peppa Hart; 54 Akila Berjaoui; 55, 58 & 60 Damian Bennett; 73 Sophie Bell; 80 Etil Thorén Due; 92 & 179 Libby Watkins; 98 pampas grass print supplied by Love your Space, flower print by Katie Clulow; 102, 113, 135, 153, 160 & 161 Vynka Hallam; 108, 110, 112, 127 & 132 Rikki Day; 118 supplied by Middle of Nowhere; 121 photographic print of skater by Camilla-Q, photographic print of palm supplied by OzDesign Furniture; 128 Ash Holmes; 156 Francesca Owen; 158 both works by Brittany Ferns; 166 & 167 Emily Abay; 175 wall hanging supplied by Pony Rider; 181 print supplied by Freedom Furniture; 182, 185, 186 & 234 Jai Vasicek; 191 & 193 both prints supplied by HK Living; 217 Craig McDean; 225 Georgie Wilson supplied by Greenhouse Interiors; 230 Carley Cornelissen; 237 supplied by Aboriginal Contemporary Gallery in Sydney, NSW; 248 Lucinda Jones.

Every reasonable effort has been made to trace the owners of copyright materials in this book, but in some instances this has proven impossible. The author(s) and publisher will be glad to receive information leading to more complete acknowledgements in subsequent printings of the book and in the meantime extend their apologies for any omissions.

ISBN 978 1 92235 157 9 Australia
ISBN 978 1 91166 828 2 UK

A catalogue record for this book is available from the National Library of Australia

A catalogue record for this book is available from the British Library
Colour reproduction by Splitting Image Colour Studio Pty Ltd, Clayton, Victoria
Printed by C&C Offset Printing Co. Ltd., China

10 9 8 7 6 5 4 3 2 1